Med

A Cookbook
Claudia Roden

Med

A Cookbook
Claudia Roden

EBURY
PRESS

For my children, Simon, Nadia and Anna; my grandchildren, Cesar, Peter, Sarah, Ruby, Nelly and Lily; and for Clive and Ros, my brother Ellis and sister-in-law Gill.

'*Cooking is the landscape in a saucepan.*'
Josep Pla

AN ADVENTURE
THAT NEVER ENDED

When my three children left home all at the same time thirty-five years ago, I decided to leave too and travel around the Mediterranean. I went alone, *a l'aventure* – without plans or arrangements.

A childhood memory lived inside me of the exhilarating moment we arrived in Alexandria by the desert road from our home in Cairo and suddenly saw the sea. To me, Alexandria was a different world, with other trees and flowers and new smells and villas painted yellow and pink. Compared to the serious and restrained Cairo, it was a city of freedom and pleasure. You felt the exuberant light-hearted mood in the cafes along the seafront. Italian, Greek and French were spoken in the street. The city was part of another world, one to which Marseille and Barcelona, Genoa, Athens and Algiers, Beirut and Tangier also belonged. That world had a culture all of its own, so powerful that the whole country was influenced as though the sea was its centre of gravity.

I wanted to find that spirit again.

Back in the 1980s, a woman travelling alone was strange and suspect, but researching food gave me a mission and a reason to be there. It allowed me to make contacts, to ask for help and to spend time in restaurant kitchens. It allowed me to accost people and introduce myself on trains, in cafés, or in the sitting rooms of *pensions*. I would start a conversation with: 'I'm an English food writer researching your cuisine. Can you tell me what your favourite dishes are?' They didn't always buy the 'English' but were always happy to talk about their food. My interest was in home cooking and regional food. I was invited into homes where people still cooked as their parents and grandparents did. Part of the pleasure of researching food was meeting people, sharing a moment of their lives and discovering their worlds. There is a special conviviality and intimacy in the kitchen that you don't quite get in the living room.

The Mediterranean has remained the focus of my work. This book is based on remembered dishes that I have encountered over decades. Working on it has kept me happy, thinking of people and places, magic moments and glorious food. It might be cold and grey and raining outside, but in my kitchen and at my desk in London I am smiling under an azure sky. The smell of garlic sizzling with crushed coriander takes me back to the Egypt of my childhood. The aroma of saffron and orange zest mingled with aniseed and garlic triggers memories of the French Riviera. I still cook the dishes in this collection for family and friends. They capture so well the special charm and spirit of a world that enthrals me.

A world of its own

The countries around the Mediterranean Sea are very different: eastern and western, Christian and Muslim, with forests, deserts, mountains, bays and islands. But they also have a lot in common. A shared climate, with hot, dry summers, mild winters and balmy air, encourages an easy-going outdoor life, alfresco eating, street foods and markets.

An incestuous history, with the same empires, occupiers, settlers and movements of populations, and an intense sea traffic and trading activities between port cities, have created a food culture that is immensely varied, unique and different from anywhere else in the world. Hospitality is an important part of that culture, and meals are a time of interaction. The custom of serving an assortment of little dishes with drinks is part of the relaxed way of life where you are supposed to enjoy the moment and the company in an unhurried way.

Every country has its own cuisine and unique dishes, and the cooking differs between town and country and from one town or village to another, but I also had a feeling of déjà vu in kitchens from one end of the sea to the other. I saw the same produce in the markets – the same vegetables, pulses and grains, the same fruits and nuts, great piles of olives, the same preserved vegetables. The meat is lamb, and also goat, hare and rabbit, with pork in Christian countries. There is not enough humidity nor the right terrain for pastures and cattle-raising so beef is not common, but chickens are plentiful and there are also ducks and migrating quails.

I saw the same utensils – clay pots that can go on top of the fire, pestles and mortars, skewers, the same wood-burning outdoor ovens. And I found similar dishes. The *brandade* of salt cod in Provence is the same as the *baccalà* of Venice or the *bacalao* of Catalonia. Chicken is cooked with grapes in Spain as it is in Tuscany. The octopus stews of Greece are like those of Provence. There are aubergine purées and broad bean purées everywhere and you also find vegetable omelettes and stuffed vegetables, rice puddings and almond pastries, sauces thickened with bread, ground almonds, pine nuts or walnuts. Tomato sauce is the signature tune of the entire Mediterranean, olives and garlic are its symbols.

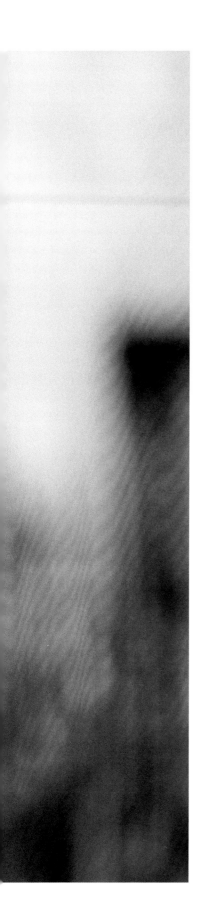

Despite the similarities, there are distinct differences. Where the French use cognac, Sicilians use Marsala and Spaniards sherry. Where Italians use mozzarella, Parmesan, pecorino or ricotta, the French use goats' cheese or Gruyère, and the Greeks, Turks, Lebanese and Egyptians use feta or halloumi. Where an Egyptian or Syrian would use ground almonds or pine nuts in a sauce, a Turk uses walnuts. Crème fraîche is used in France where yoghurt and buffalo milk cream are used in the eastern Mediterranean. In the northern Mediterranean, the flavours are of herbs that grow wild; in the eastern and southern Mediterranean they are of spices, flower waters and molasses. In Turkey they flavour their meats with cinnamon and allspice, in Morocco they use cumin, saffron, cinnamon and ginger. While a fish soup in the French Midi includes orange zest and saffron, in Tunisia it will have cumin, paprika, cayenne and coriander leaves. It's as if the common language of the Mediterranean is spoken in a myriad of dialects.

Memories of life in old rural worlds live on in the cooking, like ghosts hovering in saucepans

Many Mediterranean dishes are simple and frugal, reflecting the rural lives of people before they began leaving the land for cities, before agriculture was industrialised and tourism became the main industry, before seasonal immigrant workers did the harvesting. The old peasantry could rarely afford meat. In some countries, it was eaten only on festive occasions. In Christian countries, it was forbidden by the church on Fridays and during Lent. That is why grains, pulses, vegetables, fruit and nuts have a very important place in so many of these dishes.

An important rural tradition was the preservation of food, a means of survival when seasons alternated dramatically between short periods of great abundance and long ones of scarcity. Fruits and vegetables were laid out on trays in the fields to dry in the sun or preserved in brine or oil, or made into jams or pickles. Tomatoes were reduced to paste. Olives were cured and pickled or crushed for their oil. Grains, pulses and nuts were dried on rooftops. Meats were slowly cooked and preserved in their fat or turned into pâtés or terrines. Pork was cured and dried as ham, or made into salami. In Turkey, the Balkans and the Levant, yoghurt was drained to make a soft cheese that was rolled into balls and preserved in olive oil. The juice of sour pomegranates was boiled down to syrupy molasses. Distilled rose and orange blossom waters were produced by boiling petals in alembics. Nowadays, all these things are produced industrially and we can find them as delicacies in our supermarkets.

Sophisticated Mediterranean dishes are a legacy of a glittering past

In addition to these rural traditions, there are refinements that hark back to the powerful empires which have come and gone around the Mediterranean. The Romans spread the classical triad of bread, wine and olive oil across the entire region. The Arabs introduced irrigation techniques, new crops, horticultural and cooking practices, and brought spices and aromatics from the East. The Ummayad Caliphate, from its capital, Damascus, extended its empire through North Africa all the way to Spain. It was succeeded by the Abbasid Caliphate, whose capital was Baghdad; the grand styles of ancient Persia were adopted by the Caliphate elite and their tastes still echo in Spain, Sicily and North Africa. Among the Arab legacies are sweet-and-sour and savoury-and-sweet combinations, meats cooked with fruit, milk puddings and almond pastries. Whenever you see raisins and pine nuts in a local dish, you know that Arabs were in the region at one point.

Rich, refined dishes, developed in the court kitchens of Constantinople (now Istanbul) when it was the capital of the Ottoman Empire, appeared throughout that empire which covered much of the eastern Mediterranean and northern Africa for more than 500 years. Barcelona, once the merchant queen of the Mediterranean, had a strong influence on cooking, as had the Republic of Venice, which once had colonies and trading posts as far afield as Alexandria. And the discovery of the New World at the end of the fifteenth century brought new foods and revolutionised the Mediterranean diet. It's hard to imagine the food of the Mediterranean without tomatoes and peppers.

A book of food for family and friends

Working on this book has allowed me to keep doing what I love: cooking and spending time with friends and family. I invited two or three or four at a time to try dishes over regular little dinners around my kitchen table to find what gave us the most pleasure. I woke up excited, imagining dishes and planning menus. I devised easy meals that I could handle alone. Like everyone today, I did not want to spend hours in the kitchen and wished to enjoy the company of my friends. I wanted to please and hoped to enthral. Some of the guests at my table have been as old as I am, some were my children's and grandchildren's age. Many were vegetarian, a few were vegan, or gluten- or dairy-intolerant. I took that into consideration when planning my menus and that is reflected in my choice of recipes. I love meat, but am happier now to eat much less. The ingredients I use represent what has long been seen as the healthy 'Mediterranean diet': rich in grains, vegetables, fruit and nuts, with plenty of fish but little meat, and olive oil as the main cooking fat.

Flavours range from very delicate, through sharp, sweet-and-sour and savoury-and-sweet, to complex and spicy hot. There is almost always garlic and olive oil, often lemon and tomatoes, herbs and spices, sometimes anchovies, olives and chillies. Spirits and wines are used in the northern and western Mediterranean; aromatics such as orange blossom and rose water and pomegranate molasses are used in the east and south. Simple dishes are enlivened by sauces: extra virgin olive oil blended with garlic and a herb; versions of aïoli; nutty creams; or yoghurt with garlic, lemon or tahini.

In previous books, I have featured hundreds of traditional Middle Eastern and Mediterranean dishes that were new in Britain at the time and are now part of our modern English cuisine, with everyone doing their own take. With this book,

I wanted to offer something different. A few of the recipes are updated versions of dishes that have appeared in previous books. But the majority are entirely new. Many are French, because I have had a studio in Paris for thirty-two years, and during this time the cooking of the South became the most popular in France. There are classics and little-known traditional specialities. I have felt free to simplify and refine, to intensify flavours and make dishes more beautiful, sometimes to interpret and innovate while still keeping their traditional character.

The aim of this book is to highlight what to me is the best of the Mediterranean and adapt it for the way we like to eat today. It is what I cook when I entertain friends and family. I hope you will get as much pleasure from the dishes as we did and make them your own.

WHERE MY TASTES COME FROM

I was born in 1936. The Egypt I grew up in was a cosmopolitan world where people spoke many languages and French was the lingua franca. I lived with my parents Cesar and Nelly Douek, my brothers Ellis and Zaki, and our Slovene-Italian nanny Maria Koron, in a quarter of Cairo that was an island in the Nile called Zamalek. We were part of two large extended families. Three of my grandparents came to Egypt from Aleppo at the end of the nineteenth century when the Suez Canal was built and Egypt became a mercantile hub. My maternal grandmother was from Istanbul. Her ancestors were banished from Spain in 1492. She spoke a medieval Judeo-Spanish, but had trained as a teacher in Paris and was like a missionary for French culture. When we were small, Maria cooked for us what she knew. Awad, our cook, learned from my mother how to cook the dishes that were passed down in our families: filo cigars, *kibbeh*, *tabbouleh*, *baba ghanouj*, *konafa*, milk puddings, almond cakes – and French food.

In 1951, at fifteen, I was sent to boarding school in Paris, because Zaki had to be there after an operation and Ellis was there studying medicine. On weekends, I slept on sofas at relatives' and day girls' homes, and at the hotel Monsieur le Prince in the Latin Quarter where Ellis had a room. I hung around with friends and got to know *céleri rémoulade*, *poule au pot*, *hachis parmentier* and *chaussons aux pommes*.

I came to London to study art at Saint Martins in 1954. Ellis had also moved to medical school in London, and Zaki joined us and attended the French Lycée. We had a flat and I cooked for them and for our student friends. I spent hours rolling vine leaves and making stuffed vegetables. The only place where I could buy what I needed for our kind of food – bulgur, chickpeas, tahini,

pomegranate molasses, rose water – was at Mrs Haral's in Camden Town. In the workshop of Olympia, in Kentish Town, I could buy pitta and *kadaifi* and watch artisans make filo by hand.

I started collecting recipes in 1956, when the Jews were forced to leave Egypt after the Suez War, and my parents joined us. For many years we were inundated with refugees from Egypt passing through, looking for a country to settle in. People exchanged recipes. We thought we would never see each other again, so they were something to remember one another by. There had been no cookbooks in Egypt. What I collected was a mixed bag because the Jewish community of Egypt was a mosaic of families from all over the old Ottoman world and from around the Mediterranean.

When I married and had children, I was always trying the recipes to make them work because the instructions were not precise. 'You'll know that there is enough flour when the dough feels like your earlobe'; 'the smell will tell you when it's ready'. I went on and on collecting. I was smitten. I hung around places where I could meet people from the Middle East and ask for recipes, such as carpet warehouses and embassies. When I asked a librarian at the British Library to help me find books on Arab food, he came up with a list of translations of medieval culinary manuals. There was nothing contemporary. That is when I became interested in the history and origins of dishes and the cultures behind them.

When I decided to turn the recipes into a book and told people, they said 'Why don't you paint?' Writing about food was not the hot subject it is now. And when I said I was researching Middle Eastern dishes, they said 'is it sheeps' eyes and testicles?' *A New Book of Middle Eastern Food* and the books that followed became primary

sources for chefs and food writers discovering Middle Eastern and Mediterranean cuisines.

Writing about food was how I supported the family when my marriage split up and I became a single parent. It was the only thing I knew, but it was the most interesting, exciting thing I could do. I wrote for newspapers. I worked on the BBC TV series and book *Claudia Roden's Mediterranean Cookery*. I went to every region of Italy for *The Sunday Times Magazine*'s 'A Taste of Italy', and the book that followed. *The Book of Jewish Food* is about foods without terroir that Jews carried

in their minds as baggage from one homeland to another. Researching it and *Arabesque*, about the cooking of Morocco, Turkey and Lebanon, and then *The Food of Spain*, made me realise that food opens doors. While I was researching and recording traditional cuisines and spending time in home kitchens, I was inspired and learning from chefs who were experimenting and innovating and from those who were refining local traditions.

Working on *Med*, I revisited the tastes and joys of all the good times I had and shared them with my family and my friends.

PLANNING A MEAL

A slice of the sun and sea for family and friends

The charm of a home-cooked meal is its casual simplicity. In the Mediterranean, with its traditions of hospitality, sociability and conviviality, it is as much about the pleasures of the spirit as it is of the senses. Entertaining is a way of living that we can make our own. We may not all have the privilege of making food that is 'from the landscape to the plate', but the majority of Mediterranean ingredients are readily available to us. They may not all be as good as those grown and ripened in the sun, but we can get the best out of them.

Preparing a meal for a crowd can be hard work, but it is always worth it, and planning the menu is part of the pleasure. These days I find it useful to ask if there is anything people can't eat. I always think of having a good variety of colours, flavours, textures and nutrients with an emphasis on vegetables, pulses and grains. It is sometimes a traditional three-course meal with a soup or vegetable starter, followed by a fish, chicken, meat or vegetable main, and a sweet. Alternatively, I'll put three or more dishes that complement each other on the table. This way of serving what restaurants call 'sharing dishes' is appealing because people prefer variety above quantity. When it is just one person doing the cooking, it's not possible for them to cook too many different things and still enjoy the company. The art then is to choose, for at least part of the meal, something that is easy or that can be prepared in advance.

People are happy with a one-pot meal or a simple snack, even just a soup with bread, because you have cooked it for them. In the summer, for me, a snack might be a salad, a cold dish or an omelette; in the winter it can be a heart-warming stew or a bake. If I have all the family over, it may be a large couscous. I love dessert, but sometimes just follow with cheese and fruit. With black coffee or mint tea, I serve chocolate or Medjool dates.

Have on the table some good bread, extra virgin olive oil, flaked sea salt, a black pepper mill, and ground chilli or chilli flakes for those who always like to add it. I use the French *Piment d'Espelette* and Aleppo pepper, known as *pul biber*. Both have a rich flavour and are less hot than other ground and crushed chillies.

Choose fresh, easy, robust wines that stand up to spices and chilli, garlic, lemon and sugar: well-chilled fruity whites, rosés, dry sherries, and sparkling wines for starters and fish and summer drinking; robust reds to go with lamb, pork, chicken and also fish and cheese; a sweet wine, if you like, to serve with dessert. Keep a fine wine for the delicately flavoured dishes. The Mediterranean is wine country. There are wonderful vibrant wines from Greece, Cyprus, Turkey, Lebanon and Israel, but those from southern France, Italy and Spain are more readily available and affordable. Spirits distilled from grapes, in particular aniseed-flavoured pastis in France, arak, raki and ouzo in the eastern Mediterranean, are commonly served with chilled water (they turn cloudy white) and ice as aperitifs and are also drunk throughout the meal in the eastern Mediterranean. Beer is a good warm-weather drink, especially if you are eating outdoors. We love making sangria for a barbecue.

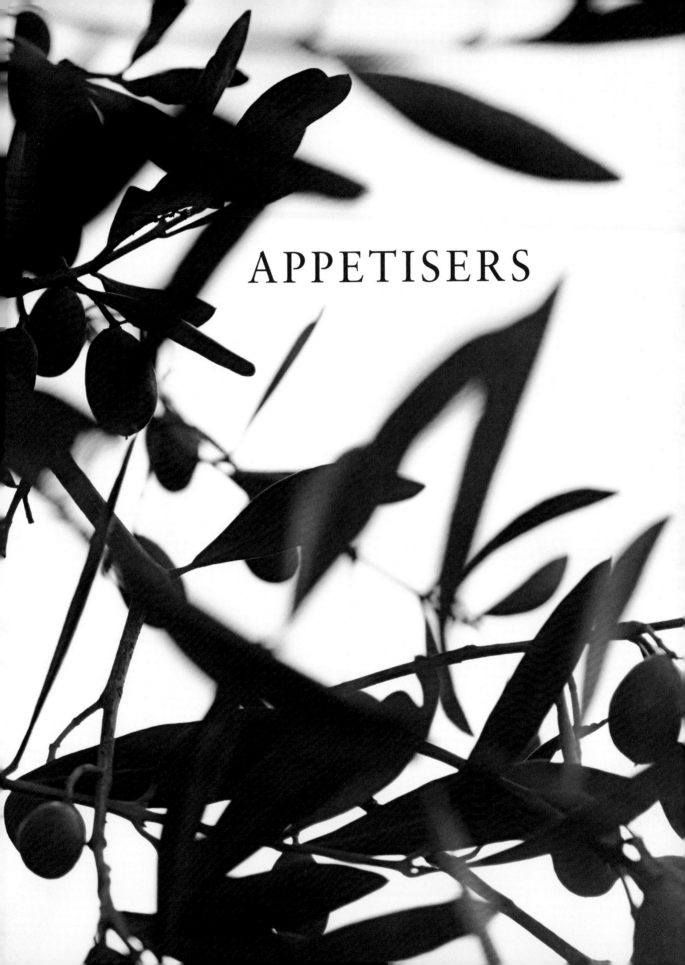

APPETISERS

The pleasure of savouring bits of food with drinks in a relaxed way in convivial company is one of the joys of Mediterranean life. It is a tradition, a ritual and an institution that was born in the world of bars, taverns and cafés. But at home, too, there are traditions of hospitality where people offer something to eat with a drink.

The appetisers I grew up with are Middle Eastern *mezze*. When my father came home from work we would sit on the balcony where we could see *felukas* (sail boats) gliding gracefully on the Nile, and Awad the cook would bring a tray of little things to eat. My parents had a glass of arak or whisky and nibbled at the food – hummus, feta cheese, olives, pickles, radishes, and the like – while we children would wolf it down before being stopped by mother because we were having dinner soon. When my parents entertained their friends to play cards, every space in the flat was filled with rented card tables, and a buffet included an enormous array of *mezze*.

I was always intrigued by the fantastical stories relatives told of a place called Zahlé, a mountain holiday resort in the Bekaa Valley in Lebanon, where they ate an incredible variety of fabulous *mezze*. That mythical place stayed in my mind and in my dreams, so you can imagine my excitement when, a few years ago, I found myself stopping in Zahlé for a *mezze* lunch on the way back to Beirut from a wedding near Baalbeck. Fergus Henderson of St. John restaurant was at the wedding with his extended family, and I got a lift with his parents, sister and the painter Ffiona Lewis. The menu was huge. I wished I could try everything. While I took notes of what we ate, Ffiona sketched the empty plates with remnants of food after we finished. A year later, she exhibited the resulting paintings (they are great) at a London gallery.

Zahlé is now a town full of concrete housing overlooked by a giant statue of the Virgin Mary perched on the mountainside. There are vineyards around and *arak* is produced. According to legend, this is where the Arab *mezze* was born, in 1920, when the first two cafés opened by the river and started serving mountain village foods with the local arak. Gradually, the entire valley became filled with open-air cafés, each larger and more luxurious than the next, each vying with ever more varied *mezze* to attract customers who flocked from all over the Middle East.

What I learned in Zahlé and elsewhere in the eastern Mediterranean and North Africa has inspired some of the dishes I serve as a first course. What I serve with drinks I have learned from people at home, usually purées or pastes on little toasts or as dips, whose rich, strong flavours are meant to open the appetite. When you have a whole meal to prepare, you don't have time for elaborate appetisers. I always have something in the fridge, such as salami or other charcuterie, some cheese to cut up and some olives and nuts, if someone should be around unexpectedly for a drink.

FOCACCIA

Of all the Mediterranean breads, focaccia (*fugassa* in the local dialect) – one of the great triumphs of Ligurian cooking – is the easiest to make at home. In Liguria, every seaside resort has its own version. The best I've eaten was in Genoa. Whenever I make it, I can't stop eating it.

Serve it cut into small squares as an antipasto and try the classic variations below.

Serves 6–8

1 tbsp (7g sachet) fast-action dried yeast
pinch of sugar
a little less than 450ml lukewarm water
750g strong white bread flour, plus extra for dusting
2 tsp salt
5 tbsp extra virgin olive oil, plus extra for greasing

Dissolve the yeast and sugar in about 100ml of the warm water and leave for about 10 minutes until it froths.

In a large bowl, mix the flour and salt and make a well in the centre. Pour in the yeast mixture and 3 tablespoons of the oil and mix with a wooden spoon. Add the remaining warm water very gradually – adding just enough to make a soft ball that holds together, mixing first with the wooden spoon, then working it in with your hand.

Turn the dough onto a lightly floured surface and knead for about 10 minutes until very smooth and elastic, adding a little flour if too sticky, or a drop of water if too dry.

Pour a little oil into the bowl and turn the dough in it to coat it all over. Cover the bowl with a clean tea towel and leave to rise in a warm place for about 1½ hours or until doubled in bulk.

Oil one or two baking tins: I use two round 28cm tins, but a large rectangular one will do very well.

Knead the dough very briefly to punch out the air, then flatten into your oiled baking tins, pressing it down with oiled hands. As the dough is very elastic and will spring back, you may need to stretch it again a few times. A focaccia can be thick or thin, so the flattened dough can be ½–1cm thick. Cover with a towel or foil and leave to rise again in a warm place for about 45 minutes.

Preheat the oven to 220°C/200°C fan/gas 7. Just before baking, use your fingers to make deep holes all over the dough and drizzle or brush with the remaining olive oil.

Cook the focaccia one tin at a time. Bake for 20 minutes or until crisp and golden on top and cooked through. It is best eaten warm, cut into squares.

Variations (before baking)

~ Sprinkle 1½ teaspoons coarse sea salt over the top.

~ Sprinkle with 2–3 chopped garlic cloves and the needles of 2 rosemary sprigs or 2 tablespoons chopped sage leaves.

~ Sprinkle with 1 tablespoon chopped oregano and 75g pitted black olives, finely chopped.

~ Brush with 3 tablespoons of tapenade (page 34).

~ Fry 2 sliced large onions in 3 tablespoons of olive oil, covered, over a very low heat, stirring occasionally, for 10–15 minutes until very soft and just beginning to colour. Season with salt and pepper. Scatter over the top.

~ Pluck 3 red piquillo peppers from a jar, cut into ribbons and scatter over the dough along with 3 chopped garlic cloves.

TARAMA

One of the joys of my days as an art student in London was dipping into a bowl of tarama with a piece of pitta at a Cypriot café called The Black Cat in Charlotte Street. It was one of a very few places where I could eat the foods of my childhood.

Tarama can be magnificent, but you must find a good source and buy really good-quality smoked cod's roe. The best type that I buy from my fishmonger is loose and pinky beige and the resulting creamy dip is ivory-coloured, not pink. I have tried the roes that are more readily available, which come vacuum-packed, look flattened and are dark orangey-brown, but they have been too salty and over-smoked. You can improve on them by soaking them in water for 2 hours, changing the water a couple of times. This will also make them easier to skin.

When we get together these days, we rely on my son Simon to make the tarama. His is always marvellous, with a delicate fishy flavour, because he has a good source for the roe. This is his recipe, but he makes it to taste and keeps adding olive oil and lemon juice until satisfied.

Serve it as a dip with warmed pitta bread cut into triangles with scissors, or thin toast.

Serves 8

½ lobe (about 270g) smoked cod's roe

2 small garlic cloves, crushed

5 tbsp lemon juice, or more to taste

100ml sunflower oil

2 tbsp extra virgin olive oil, or more to taste

Skin the smoked cod's roe, if it's easy to do so: I don't always manage to get all the skin off and it's fine. Put it in a food processor, add the garlic and lemon juice, and blend until smooth.

Gradually add the sunflower oil and olive oil in a thin trickle while the blades are running and blend to the consistency of a thick mayonnaise. Taste and add more lemon juice or olive oil, if you like.

Scrape into a bowl, cover, and chill in the fridge, where it will firm up, before serving.

TAPENADE

Black olive, caper and anchovy paste

Travelling south in France, I felt, at a certain point, that I had opened a door into another world. The sky was different, the light and colours and smells were different, the architecture and vegetation were different – and there were olive trees. This famous paste consists mostly of olives but takes its name from the old Provençal word for caper, *tapeno*. It is the ideal appetiser, but you must use good-quality olives such as Kalamata, which are now readily available, pitted, in jars. The rum or brandy makes it special. Spread it on toast or serve as a dip. I use any left over as a sauce for pasta. It keeps in the fridge for at least 2 weeks.

Serves 8–10

290g jar (160g drained weight) good-quality pitted black olives, such as Kalamata

2 tbsp capers in brine, squeezed

3 anchovy fillets in oil, drained

1 garlic clove, crushed (optional)

3 tbsp rum or brandy, to taste (optional)

2–3 tbsp extra virgin olive oil

Using a hand blender, blend all the ingredients together to form a smooth paste.

FRESH GOATS' CHEESE WITH HERBS AND OLIVES

One summer, when my children were small, we camped at Lacoste in the Vaucluse in the South of France. My art school friend, the late Dutch sculptress Ans Hey, was building a house on the side of a hill with the help of her Amsterdam colleagues and students. I helped with the cooking. The area was blanketed with a scrub full of fragrant wild herbs. Every day, the children were sent off to gather some to throw in the fire under a huge grill where meat was roasting, or to put in a salad, omelette or stew. We would mash some into the fresh goats' cheeses we bought at the weekly farmers' markets, sometimes adding a little of the pastis we were drinking.

At home in London, I use other anise-flavoured spirits such as arak, or sometimes rum. I buy alcoholic spirits mainly for cooking. It is worth investing in a few as they have an important place in northern Mediterranean cooking.

Serve on toast or as a dip.

Makes 8–10 toasts

150g fresh goats' cheese

1½ tbsp extra virgin olive oil

1 tbsp pastis, arak, raki or ouzo – or white rum (optional)

1 small garlic clove, crushed (optional)

freshly ground black pepper, to taste

1 tbsp snipped fresh chives or chopped dill, to garnish

5 pitted black olives, chopped, to garnish

Using a fork, mash the goats' cheese with the oil, pastis and garlic, if using, and season with a little pepper.

Spread on little toasts and garnish with a sprinkling of herbs and olives, or serve as a dip for sticks of raw vegetables, such as cucumber or carrot.

Pictured on page 34.

MUHAMMARA WALNUT AND ROAST PEPPER DIP

This dip can be mild, as it is in Syria, or very hot with lots of chilli, as I had it in Gaziantep in Turkey. The city of Gaziantep was once part of Syria, where my great-grandfather Haham Abraham ha Cohen Douek was a young rabbi (in what was then Antep) before he became Chief Rabbi of Aleppo. I keep a portrait of him in my kitchen, in a kaftan and turban and wearing the medals pinned on him by Sultan Abdul Hamid II. When my family moved to Cairo they brought the tastes of Aleppo with them.

My own version is very easy to make, using a jar of roasted and peeled piquillo peppers from Spain, which you will find in supermarkets. Garnish the muhammara, if you like, with walnut halves or pomegranate seeds. Serve it on toast or in Little Gem lettuce leaves.

Serves 8

320g jar red piquillo peppers
100g walnut halves
1 slice (about 30g) of wholemeal bread, crusts removed
2 garlic cloves, crushed
1–1½ tbsp pomegranate molasses
juice of ½ lemon
3–4 tbsp extra virgin olive oil
1½ tsp ground cumin
¼–½ tsp Aleppo pepper or other hot chilli pepper
salt, to taste

Drain the peppers well and put them in a food processor with the remaining ingredients. Blend to a thick, coarse paste.

Spread the paste in a serving dish or spoon it into Little Gem lettuce leaves.

AUBERGINE PURÉE

I love the creamy flesh and slightly bitter smoky taste of roasted aubergines with just olive oil and lemon. It is for good reason that in France it is known as *caviar d'aubergines*. Variations of this purée are found all round the Mediterranean. Serve it as a dip or spread on toast.

Serves 4–6

3 aubergines, trimmed and cut in half lengthways
4 tbsp extra virgin olive oil, plus extra for greasing
juice of ½–1 lemon, or more to taste
salt and black pepper

Preheat the grill to high. Line a baking sheet with foil, brush it with oil and add the aubergines, cut-side down. Cook under the grill for 20–25 minutes until the skins are black and blistered and the aubergines feel very soft inside when you press them. (Alternatively, preheat the oven to 220°C/200°C fan/gas 7; prick the whole aubergines in a few places with a pointed knife so they don't burst, and roast them for about 45 minutes, turning them at least once.)

When cool enough to handle, use a spoon to scoop out the flesh into a colander and gently press to get rid of some of the juices. Chop the flesh with a sharp knife and then mash it with a fork.

In a serving bowl, beat the oil with the lemon juice and some salt and pepper, and mix in the mashed aubergines.

Variations

~ For the Levantine *baba ghanouj*, beat 4 tablespoons of tahini with 2 tablespoons water and the juice of 1 lemon (the tahini stiffens at first, then softens), then beat in the mashed aubergines. Season with salt and pepper and add 1 or 2 crushed garlic cloves. Before serving, stir in 2 tablespoons chopped flat-leaf parsley.

~ For Turkish *buran*, mix the mashed aubergines with 250g Greek-style yoghurt, the juice of 1 lemon, 1 crushed garlic clove and salt to taste.

~ For a Syrian version, mix the mashed aubergines with 2 tablespoons pomegranate molasses, 1 tablespoon lemon juice, 2 tablespoons extra virgin olive oil, salt and pepper.

~ For a spicy Moroccan version, add 1 crushed garlic clove, a good pinch of chilli pepper, ½ teaspoon ground cumin and 1 tablespoon chopped coriander leaves.

LABNEH

This thick, velvety drained yoghurt makes a wonderfully refreshing side dish. There are few things it doesn't go with. It is my little luxury to eat it, without salt, just by itself. A traditional way of draining the yoghurt is to hang it in a long cloth set over a bowl, but I leave it in a colander. I serve it as a *mezze* with a drizzle of extra virgin olive oil and any of these – sumac, chilli, crushed garlic, dried mint, grated lemon zest, snipped fresh chives or chopped dill – not all at once. Serve it with warmed triangles of pitta bread or sticks of raw cucumber and carrot.

Serves 8

450g Greek-style yoghurt
¼–⅓ teaspoon fine sea salt (optional)

Line a colander with a clean cloth (such as a napkin, a piece of muslin or cheesecloth, or a J-cloth) and place it in a bowl so that it doesn't touch the bottom. Pour in the yoghurt (if you want it salty, beat in the fine sea salt first) and bring up the corners of the cloth to cover it.

Put the bowl in the fridge and leave it overnight, or longer. The liquid whey will drain away; you will have to pour it out occasionally. The longer you leave it, the thicker it gets.

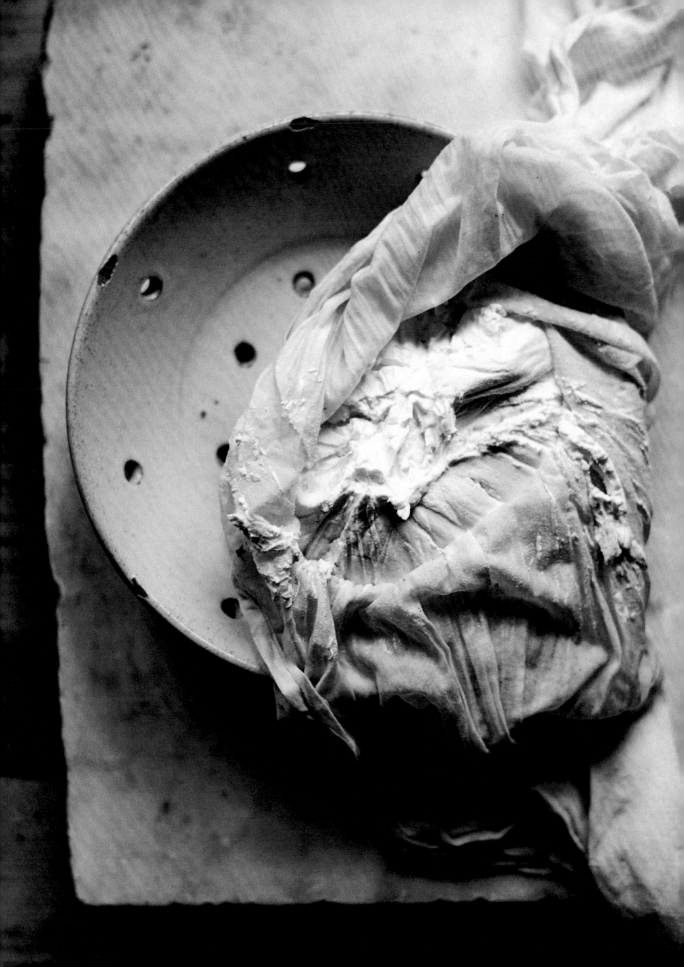

ROASTED CHEESE POLENTA CUBES

It is amazing how polenta keeps reinventing itself. Originally the despised porridge of a desperately poor northern Italian peasantry, it appeared in restaurants in the 1980s as a thin, grilled triangle or as a creamy base for elegant food. I can never make enough of these heavenly bites, crisp and golden on the outside and soft inside. Everyone adores them. You can make the polenta the day before, then cut it into cubes and roast them just before serving. My son Simon has adopted these as a side dish for, say, sausages, in which case the cubes should be cut a little bigger.

Makes about 32

1 litre water

2 tsp salt

250g instant polenta

75g Parmesan or Grana Padano, grated

100g semi-soft cheese such as Fontina or Taleggio, cut into pieces

3 tsp chopped rosemary leaves

freshly ground black pepper, to taste

at least 4 tbsp olive or sunflower oil

Bring the water to the boil with the salt in a very large pan. Pour in the polenta, beating vigorously with a whisk. When it comes back to the boil, reduce the heat and continue to stir with the whisk for 3 minutes, making sure that no lumps form. It will gurgle and splatter, so you might need to put a cloth around your hand. Add both cheeses, the rosemary and some pepper and whisk well to make sure the cheese melts evenly. Cover the pan and cook over very low heat for 8 minutes, stirring occasionally.

Line a 30 x 20cm tray with foil – if you have a larger tray, line it with foil that you can fold up to contain the polenta in a layer about 2.5cm thick. Brush with oil. Pour the polenta into the tray, let it cool, then cover and leave in the fridge for at least 2 hours.

Half an hour before serving, preheat the oven to 240°C/220°C fan/gas 9.

Cut the polenta into cubes with a sharp knife. Pour the remaining oil into another, larger, baking dish or roasting tin, and tip the polenta cubes out into it, then turn them in the oil to coat them on all sides. Roast for 20–25 minutes until nicely crisp and golden, turning them over once. Serve hot.

GREEN OLIVE, WALNUT AND POMEGRANATE SALAD

This little salad, a thrilling mix of flavours, textures and colours that is almost too glorious to look at, is a speciality of Gaziantep, a Turkish city on the border with Syria, famous for its gastronomy. If you don't have pomegranate seeds, never mind.

Serves 4

100g good-quality pitted green olives in brine, drained

50g walnuts

3 spring onions, chopped

bunch (25g) of flat-leaf parsley, leaves chopped

2 tbsp extra virgin olive oil

1 tbsp lemon juice

2 tbsp pomegranate molasses

salt, to taste

chilli flakes, to taste

3 tbsp pomegranate seeds

Coarsely chop the olives and walnuts, place in a serving dish and mix with the spring onions and parsley.

In a small bowl, mix the olive oil, lemon juice and pomegranate molasses with a little salt and chilli flakes to taste. Pour over the olives and walnuts and sprinkle with pomegranate seeds.

CHICKEN LIVER MOUSSE

A tiny tartlet filled with an exquisite chicken liver mousse was part of an assortment of Alain Ducasse's canapés I was offered when I interviewed the great chef at his Michelin 3-star restaurant in Paris. The sweet and fortified wines give mine a sumptuous flavour. I serve it on lightly toasted brioche bread, sometimes with a teaspoon of fruit preserve such as quince or apricot beside it. Make it at least 3 hours before serving, and leave to firm up in the fridge.

Serves 6

400g chicken livers

25g unsalted butter

2 garlic cloves, crushed

1 tsp thyme leaves

4 tbsp sweet Marsala or muscatel wine

2 tbsp brandy or ruby port

100ml double cream

salt and black pepper

Chicken livers are generally sold cleaned, but check them over and trim off any sinews or greenish bits.

Melt the butter in a large frying pan, add the livers and cook over high heat for 2 minutes, with the garlic, thyme and some salt and pepper, turning them until browned all over but still a little bloody inside. Pour in the sweet wine and let it bubble and evaporate over medium heat for a minute or so – the chicken livers should still be pink inside.

Tip the livers with the pan juices into a food processor, add the brandy or port, then blend to a paste. Whip the cream until thick, then add it to the food processor and blend to a creamy consistency. Taste and adjust the seasoning. Scrape into a bowl and leave, covered, in the fridge for a few hours.

Serve on toasted slices of brioche.

SOUPS

When I first moved into my little studio in Paris, in the long cobbled courtyard that had once been stables, the first thing I did was to buy pots and pans and kitchen utensils. I went to the flea market and bought a small country table (they called it a wine-tasting table) and four wooden chairs. It was 1989. I phoned relatives and friends and started inviting people to eat. I took my basket on wheels to the Rue Cler street market, filled it with goodies and went home to cook. I was ecstatic. But I soon stopped making dinners in my tiny kitchen because I wanted to be out and about meeting friends, researching at libraries, seeing exhibitions, browsing in bookshops, going to events. Paris is a city where so much is going on and it feels good just to wander around the streets. The name of a street, the sight of a restaurant or a café, brought back memories of the times we came on holiday with my parents and when I was at school. I would sit in a café, order a coffee or a soup, read my paper and dream.

Soup is everyone's comfort food and it is mine. At one time, I took lunch breaks in a little restaurant that specialised in healthy vegetarian food. Every day they made a different cream of vegetable soup, a *velouté de légumes*, which could be pumpkin, carrots, leeks, mushrooms, cauliflower, peas. In the past, they might have forced the soup through a food mill, now they blended it in a food processor. Some are nostalgic for the old way.

When I asked a sociologist friend about the *cuisines des terroirs*, he said: 'They exist only in cookery books.' You might not find regional dishes in their regions, but I have found them in Paris, in bistros and restaurants and in people's homes. Much of the population of the capital comes from the regions and some keep up family traditions.

When I first came to Paris, the food of the Midi (Southern France) was not valued. It was even despised and considered not properly French, because there were so many foreign influences: Spanish, Arab, Italian. However, now it is the most popular for its strong flavours, spices and perfumes and its use of olive oil. It is what people want to eat and the inspiration for influential avant-garde chefs like Alain Ducasse. *La cuisine du soleil*, also called *la cuisine des epices*, is in its golden age.

When I started thinking of soups for this book, I went through all the ones I had eaten and loved around the Mediterranean for inspiration. There were many. What you have here are my favourites. They make an easy and delightful first course. You will find splendid fish soups, that are the heart and soul of the Mediterranean, in the fish and seafood chapter (page 171).

GAZPACHO ANDALUZ

This is the best thing you can have in the summer, when tomatoes are sweet and full of flavour. When I stayed with Manolo el Sereno in Frailes, a village in Andalusia, I helped him make enough gazpacho to fill half a dozen giant Coca-Cola bottles. He told me of the time when, from the age of seven, he worked on an estate, looking after the mules and helping to make food for the seasonal labourers. When they worked in the vegetable gardens, they took *dornillos* (large mortars) to pound the ingredients for gazpacho, along with olive oil, salt, vinegar and some bread. Manolo was the president of the gastronomic guild of the region of Jaén. It was their festival and everyone brought food. A band played flamenco and people got up to sing of the pain and joys of those who once worked on the land.

Serves 6–8

1 slice (about 50g) of good white bread, crusts removed (optional)

1kg ripe plum tomatoes

1 green or red pepper, seeded and cut into pieces

1 cucumber, peeled and cut into pieces

2 garlic cloves, crushed

3 tbsp sherry vinegar or wine vinegar, or more to taste

4 tbsp extra virgin olive oil, plus 3 tbsp to serve

1 tsp sugar, or more to taste

salt and black pepper

If using bread, preheat the grill to low and put the bread under the grill to dry out without browning it, turning once. Break it up into pieces.

Wash the tomatoes, then quarter them and remove the little white hard bits at the stem end.

Blend the pepper to a paste in a food processor (a green pepper gives a more zingy flavour, a red one is sweeter). Add the rest of the ingredients and blend to a light creamy consistency. Pour into a serving bowl, cover and chill in the fridge for at least 1 hour.

Check the seasoning and serve in soup bowls. Drizzle a little extra virgin olive oil over each serving.

YOGHURT SOUP WITH ORZO AND CHICKPEAS

This splendid, delicately flavoured soup is inspired by one that charmed me completely at a dinner in Istanbul to celebrate the adoption by UNESCO of Gaziantep as a Creative City for its gastronomy. All the recipes on the menu hailed from the city. You must try it – it's marvellous. My granddaughter Ruby, who tested it, has adopted it with her friends at university. She sent me a photo of them eating it at their kitchen table with antique candlesticks and a bottle of wine.

The egg yolk and cornflour prevent the yoghurt from curdling as it cooks. The tiny pasta called orzo (or you can use long grain rice) are cooked separately and added just before serving: if left in the soup too long they become bloated and mushy.

Serves 4

50g orzo or long grain rice

700ml chicken or vegetable stock

1 tbsp cornflour

1 egg yolk

250g Greek-style yoghurt

1 tbsp dried mint

good pinch of saffron threads or ½ tsp ground turmeric

120g tinned chickpeas, drained and rinsed

salt and black pepper

To garnish (*optional*)

extra virgin olive oil

sumac

chilli pepper

Cook the orzo or rice in boiling salted water for about 10 minutes until done (check the packet instructions) and then drain. At the same time, bring the stock to the boil in a separate pan.

In a bowl, beat the cornflour and egg yolk together with a fork until smooth, then beat in a ladleful of the yoghurt until well blended. You can then add the remaining yoghurt and beat until combined. Stir in the mint, saffron or turmeric and some pepper.

Take the stock off the heat and pour in the yoghurt mixture, whisking vigorously. Stir over very low heat until the soup begins to simmer. Continue to stir for 3–5 minutes until it thickens slightly, then add the chickpeas and heat through. Add a little salt to taste.

A few minutes before serving, mix the cooked orzo or rice into the soup.

Serve with extra virgin olive oil, sumac and chilli for people to sprinkle on the soup if they want to.

CHILLED CREAM OF BEETROOT AND YOGHURT SOUP

This wonderfully refreshing and tasty electric-pink soup is inspired by a Turkish salad. The earthy sweetness of the beetroots marries well with the slightly tart creamy yoghurt. You must use fresh young beetroots that are sold in bunches with their leaves on.

Serves 6–8

6 medium beetroots (about 750g total weight)

700ml water

350g full-fat natural yoghurt

juice of 1 lemon

salt, to taste

4 tbsp chopped fresh dill or chives, to garnish

Wash the beetroots and cut off the leaves, then peel them, cut them in half and put them in a large pan with the water. Bring to the boil, then simmer, with the lid on, for 30–40 minutes until very tender. Leave to cool and then blend in a food processor until smooth.

Add the yoghurt, lemon juice and salt to taste and blend to a light creamy consistency. Serve sprinkled with dill or chives.

CREAM OF GREEN PEA SOUP WITH PISTOU

My Mediterranean addition to this homely, velvety soup is a drizzle of the Provençal sauce *pistou*, the French version of the pesto found across the border in Liguria. It adds flavour and richness. When I make this, I think of my friend the late Mireille Johnston, who presented the BBC TV series *A Cook's Tour of France* in the early 1990s. She lived with her husband and two daughters round the corner from my little studio in Paris. She would call and say *'On t'attend pour la soupe'* (we're expecting you for the soup) – *la soupe* was an entire meal. She was born in Nice and had a special love for what she called the 'cuisine of the sun'.

Serves 4

2 tbsp olive oil

1 onion, chopped

2 garlic cloves, chopped

400g frozen peas

600ml chicken or vegetable stock

100ml double cream

salt and black pepper

Pistou

bunch (30g) of basil, leaves only

1–1½ garlic cloves, crushed

40g Parmesan, grated

3 tbsp extra virgin olive oil

First, make the pistou. Using a hand blender, blend all the ingredients together to make a thick paste.

Heat the oil in a pan over medium heat. Add the onion and garlic and fry, stirring often, for 3–4 minutes, until softened.

Add the frozen peas and stock and bring to the boil. Reduce the heat and simmer for 7–10 minutes until the peas are soft.

Add the cream, then blend the soup and season to taste. Reheat if necessary and add a tablespoon or so of pistou to each serving.

EGYPTIAN RED LENTIL SOUP

I travelled along the Nile to research the peasant food and to interview chefs in tourist hotels before a seminar I was giving for the Association of Egyptian Chefs. In a little village, seeing me walk past her house, a woman invited me in and offered me lentil soup. It was the type of spicy, creamy, comfort food that I love. Later, at the seminar in the ballroom of the Marriot Hotel (a former palace in the Zamalek district of Cairo where I used to live), I told the chefs to put lentil soup on their menus.

Serves 6–8

1 large onion, chopped

1 carrot, finely chopped

4–5 garlic cloves, finely chopped

3 tbsp olive oil

300g split red lentils

2 litres chicken or vegetable stock

1½–2 tsp ground cumin

1½ tsp ground coriander

good pinch of chilli pepper (optional)

juice of 1 lemon

salt and black pepper

Soften the onion, carrot and garlic in the oil in a large pan over low heat for about 10 minutes.

Add the lentils and stock, bring to the boil and skim off the foam that forms at the top, then simmer for 30–40 minutes, until the lentils have disintegrated.

Stir in the cumin, coriander, chilli, if using, and lemon juice and season to taste. Simmer for 5 minutes more. If the soup needs thinning – it should not be too thick – add a little water and bring to the boil again. Serve hot.

Caramelised onion garnish (optional)

In a large frying pan, fry 2 or 3 large sliced onions in 3–4 tablespoons olive or sunflower oil, covered, over low heat for 20–30 minutes, stirring often until they are very soft. Remove the lid, raise the heat to medium and cook, stirring often, for about 15 minutes until the onions are really dark brown and caramelised. Add a good tablespoon to each serving of soup.

EGG AND LEMON CHICKEN SOUP

My version of the sharp, creamy Greek *avgolemono* soup is a light meal in itself, with chunks of chicken and rice or orzo. Using chicken with bone and skin gives it a little fat and more flavour. You can prepare the soup in advance and whisk in the egg and lemon mixture just before serving. Serve the rice separately so that people can say how much of it they want in the soup.

Serves 4

1 litre good chicken stock (home-made or good-quality bought)

3 fat chicken thighs, bone in, skin on

125g long grain rice or orzo

2 large eggs

3 tbsp lemon juice

1 tbsp finely chopped flat-leaf parsley

salt and black pepper

Put the stock and the chicken thighs in a large pan. Bring to the boil, skim off the foam that forms at the top, add salt and pepper and then turn down the heat, cover and simmer over low heat for about 25 minutes until the thighs are very tender. Lift them out and leave until cool enough to handle. Remove the skin and bones, cut the meat into largish pieces and put it back into the stock.

In another pan, bring plenty of salted water to the boil and add the rice or orzo. Cook for about 10 minutes until done (check the packet instructions) and then drain quickly.

Just before you are ready to serve, return the stock to a simmer. Beat the eggs vigorously in a bowl, then beat in the lemon juice. Gradually add 2 ladlefuls of the simmering soup, beating constantly. Pour this back into the soup, beating vigorously. Take off the heat quickly or the eggs will curdle.

Serve immediately, sprinkled with the parsley.

PUMPKIN SOUP WITH ORZO AND AMARETTI

The pumpkins of the city of Mantua in northern Italy (called *capello del prete* because they look like a priest's hat) are celebrated for their exceptionally sweet and delicate flavour, and the city is famous for its pumpkin *risotti* and *tortelli*. This soup is inspired by the filling in the *tortelli di zucca* I ate there. If you don't have a fine-tasting pumpkin, use butternut squash.

You can prepare the soup in advance, but cook the pasta separately when reheating the soup and add it just before serving.

Serves 6–8

800g pumpkin or butternut squash, peeled and cut into pieces
500ml water, plus 2 chicken or vegetable stockpots or cubes
150g orzo
500ml whole milk
salt and black pepper

To serve

ground cinnamon
grated Parmesan
9 crunchy (not chewy) amaretti biscuits, roughly crushed

Put the pumpkin or squash in a pan with the water and stockpots or cubes. Bring to the boil then simmer, covered, over low heat for 20 minutes until the pumpkin is soft.

At the same time cook the orzo in boiling salted water for about 10 minutes until al dente, and drain quickly.

Blend the pumpkin or squash to a purée using a hand blender (or in a food processor) then add the milk. Bring to a simmer, taking care not to let it boil over, and season to taste with salt and pepper.

Just before serving, bring the soup to a simmer and add the cooked orzo. Pass around little bowls of cinnamon, grated Parmesan and crumbled amaretti for your guests to sprinkle over their soup.

SALADS AND COLD VEGETABLE DISHES

A fresh leaf salad with fruit and perhaps a soft goats' cheese is a delightful way to start a meal. Vegetables cooked in oil to be served cold, a culinary style of the Mediterranean, also make a perfect first course. The advantage, for me, is that they can be made in advance, and any leftovers can be offered from the fridge as an appetiser with drinks, a day or two later. I also make a casual summer meal of one or two cold vegetable dishes, accompanied by cheese or charcuterie and some good bread.

You can use various oils for cooking – I use olive oil or sunflower – but for dressing leaf salads and for drizzling on cooked vegetables, it has to be extra virgin olive oil. For salad leaves, I use a fruity, mild, delicate, fragrant extra virgin; to drizzle over cooked vegetables, depending on the vegetable, it can sometimes be a strong-tasting, bitter, spicy oil.

While hot vegetables are enhanced by herbs, cold vegetables and grain salads do well with spices too, and with sharp or sweet-and-sour dressings and garnishes such as olives, capers and anchovies, nuts and pomegranate seeds. In the Arab world, a certain magic surrounds the use of spices and aromatics, which are used for their flavour and are also believed to have medicinal, therapeutic and even sometimes aphrodisiac value. In local folklore, they are variously believed to increase the appetite, help digestion or calm the nerves, to be good for the heart and circulation, to be anti-toxic or sexually stimulating and even to kill microbes. Cumin is said to open the appetite, ginger to make people loving, rose water to give a rosy outlook, dill and aniseed to have digestive qualities, and garlic to be both health-giving and antiseptic – attributes that may be well founded or romantic.

I used to bring back bags of spices and aromatics from souks and bazaars. Now, I find all that I need for cooking in London.

A taste that I love for cold vegetables is that of sweet-and-sour, obtained with lemon or vinegar and sugar or honey, or with pomegranate molasses. You find it right across the region. It is a legacy from medieval Baghdad. Chefs in Andalusia tell you that it was introduced there by a lute player from Baghdad known as Ziryab, who fled from the court of Harun al-Rashid and joined the court of Córdoba. When the Queen Elizabeth Hall at the Southbank Centre in London put on a series of concerts called 'Words and Music', they asked me to join a Spanish flamenco player and a lute player from Baghdad in an event they advertised as 'A Night in Andalusia'. I was to talk about my experiences of food in Andalusia between their pieces. I agreed with the flamenco player that I should talk about Ziryab, who is credited by musicians for introducing new music in Spain. Ziryab means blackbird – he had a dark complexion and is said to have sung like a bird. I think of him when I make aubergines in a spicy honey sauce (page 106). Do try it.

Whenever you are after a sweet-and-sour or a savoury-and-sweet taste, and when you are using spices and aromatics, it is best to start with little and then add more and adjust the balance after you taste, because ingredients vary as products of nature, and spices also depend on their age. Market brands also differ in strength for products such as rose and orange blossom water and pomegranate molasses. Trust your taste. If you like something, then the flavouring is right.

CITRUS SALAD WITH GREEN LEAVES

In Taormina, in Sicily, I visited a ceramicist who had created a ceramic orchard of life-size orange and lemon trees. I still have the plates I bought from him and I have never forgotten the salad we ate sitting among the glittering trees. This salad is inspired by his. I serve it as a first course with bread, sometimes after a main course, or as part of a group of three or more 'sharing' dishes that I put on the table together. It brings a tangy freshness to a meal.

The salad leaves could be a mix of two or three varieties, some mild, some spicy or bitter, such as Little Gem lettuce leaves, pea shoots, lamb's lettuce, watercress, curly endive or rocket. You could also toss some chopped herbs in with them.

Serves 6

1 large grapefruit
1 large sweet orange (a blood orange is nice)
150–200g small salad leaves
good handful of fresh mixed herbs such as chives, dill and flat-leaf parsley, chopped
juice of ½ lemon
4 tbsp extra virgin olive oil
salt and black pepper

Peel the fruits using a serrated knife: slice off the tops, then cut down the sides, making sure you remove the pith with the peel. Then, cut them into slices and arrange them on a wide platter.

Arrange the salad leaves and herbs on top. Mix the lemon juice and olive oil with some salt and pepper and pour this dressing all over the salad.

ROCKET WITH PANCETTA AND GRAPES

I love the combination of hot, crisp, salty pancetta and soft, juicy, sweet grapes with the slightly bitter fresh leaves. You can fry the pancetta and grapes in advance and reheat them just before serving.

Serves 4–6

3 tbsp olive or sunflower oil, for cooking

150g cubed pancetta

200g red or black grapes

65g rocket leaves

3 tbsp extra virgin olive oil

1 tbsp lemon juice or white wine vinegar

salt and black pepper

Heat 1 tablespoon of the oil in a small frying pan over medium heat, add the pancetta and fry for 8–10 minutes, stirring until the pancetta releases plenty of fat and becomes crisp. Drain on kitchen paper.

At the same time, heat the remaining 2 tablespoons of oil in another frying pan and fry the grapes, gently stirring until they are soft and caramelised.

Spread the rocket leaves in a wide serving dish and dress with the extra virgin olive oil, lemon juice and a sprinkling of salt and pepper. Scatter the grapes and pancetta over the salad.

FENNEL WITH PEACHES AND FRESH GOATS' CHEESE

The sweet taste and floral scent of peaches go very well with the creamy fresh goats' cheese, fennel and cucumber in this glorious salad. The peaches should be ripe but not soft – marinating them for an hour in the dressing will soften them. Put the other ingredients together at the last minute.

Serves 6–8

3 large orange-fleshed peaches

2 tbsp lemon juice

6 tbsp extra virgin olive oil

1 large fennel bulb or 2 small ones

2 small cucumbers, peeled and sliced

250g mild soft fresh goats' cheese, cut into 6–8 pieces

salt and black pepper

Drop the peaches into boiling water for a few seconds, then drain and leave until cool enough to handle. Peel them, cut them in half and then cut each half into slices (three to six slices, depending on how many people you are serving), removing the stones. Put them in a bowl.

Make a dressing with the lemon juice, olive oil and some salt and pepper. Pour 2 tablespoons of the dressing over the peaches and mix well. Leave them for about 1 hour, turning them in the dressing at least once before serving. Set the remaining dressing aside.

Trim the ends of the fennel and remove any tough outer leaves. Keep any feathery fronds and cut the fennel into very thin, long slices using a sharp knife.

Just before serving put the fennel and cucumber on a wide serving plate and toss in the remaining dressing. Add the peaches and goats' cheese and pour over the juices from the peaches. Sprinkle on the feathery fennel fronds.

Variation

Instead of fennel, use salad leaves, a mix of two or three of the following – lettuce, curly endive (frisée), lamb's lettuce, rocket.

CUCUMBER AND TOMATO SALAD

This is my simple everyday salad, as my mother always made it. If I have herbs in the fridge, I put some in. I sometimes add feta cheese.

Serves 4

4 small cucumbers, peeled and cut into 1cm-thick slices, or 1 long one, peeled, cut in half lengthways and then sliced

5 plum tomatoes, cut into wedges

5 spring onions, thinly sliced

3 tbsp extra virgin olive oil

juice of ½ lemon

small handful of 1 or 2 fresh herbs such as flat-leaf parsley, oregano, dill, chives, chervil, coriander, chopped (optional)

100g feta cheese, cut into chunks (optional)

salt and black pepper

Put the cucumbers, tomatoes and spring onions in a bowl.

Make a dressing with the oil, lemon juice and some salt and pepper.

Just before serving, pour the dressing over the salad and mix well. Sprinkle on the herbs and add feta, if you like.

SWEET AND SOUR PEPERONATA

On arrival in Palermo, as a guest of a cruise ship doing the Sicilian volcanic islands, the first dinner was in an aristocrat's ancient palazzo. The aristocrat's much younger Austrian wife sang operatic pieces. It was billed as a *monsu* dinner (the word is derived from 'monsieur', after the French chefs who came to cook for the Sicilian aristocracy after the French Revolution). I have adopted their voluptuous *peperonata in agrodolce* and serve it as a first course or side dish or as an antipasto, spread on crostini.

Serves 4–6

3 large fleshy peppers (red, orange, yellow), seeded

5 tbsp olive oil

2 red onions, halved and sliced

4 garlic cloves, peeled

1 tbsp sugar or honey

3 tbsp white or red wine vinegar

salt and black pepper

Optional garnishes

6 anchovy fillets in oil, drained

6 pitted black olives

1 tbsp drained capers

sprigs of basil or mint, leaves torn

Cut the peppers into ribbons.

Heat the oil in a large frying pan or sauté pan, put in the onions, garlic and peppers, season with salt and pepper and cook over low heat, covered, stirring occasionally, for 30–40 minutes, until they are very soft.

Dissolve the sugar or honey in the vinegar, pour over the peppers and stir well. Cook for another 5–10 minutes.

Serve at room temperature. Garnish, if you like, with anchovy fillets, olives and capers and sprinkle with basil or mint.

RED PEPPER AND TOMATO SALAD

Inspired by Moroccan cooked salads, this one is a favourite for its glorious colour and marvellous flavours. The addition of boiled lemon, with its unique sharp taste, is my little 'fantasia'. For this, boil an unwaxed lemon for 30 minutes until it is very soft.

Serves 4–6

3 large fleshy red peppers

1½ tbsp olive oil

300g cherry or baby plum tomatoes, such as Santini

½–1 fresh chilli, seeded and chopped, or a good pinch of ground chilli (optional)

3 garlic cloves, finely chopped

½ tsp sugar

1 small boiled lemon (see above) or ½ large one (optional)

3–4 tbsp extra virgin olive oil

a few sprigs of coriander, leaves chopped

salt

Preheat the oven to 220°C/200°C fan/gas 7 and line a baking sheet with baking parchment or foil. Cut the peppers in half through the stalks, remove the stalks, seeds and membranes and arrange them, cut-side down, on the baking sheet. Roast for 25–35 minutes until they are soft and their skin is blistered. Put them in an empty pan with a tight-fitting lid or in a bowl with a plate on top and leave them to steam for 10 minutes, which will loosen the skins. When cool enough to handle, peel off the skins and cut each half into four ribbons.

While the peppers are roasting, heat the oil in a frying pan and add the tomatoes and chilli, if using. Cook over low heat for 10 minutes, shaking the pan and turning the tomatoes over with a spatula until they are soft. Push them to the side of the pan, add the garlic to an empty bit of the pan and cook, stirring, until the aroma rises and the garlic just begins to colour. Add the sugar and some salt and stir well.

Add the peppers to the tomatoes. If using the lemon, cut it into small pieces and add it to the pan, juice and all, but removing the pips. Stir gently over low heat for a minute or so. Leave to cool.

Serve at room temperature, drizzled with plenty of extra virgin olive oil and a sprinkling of coriander.

Variations

~ Garnish with 10 black olives and 10 anchovy fillets in oil.

~ For Neapolitan *peperoni e pomodorini in agrodolce*, dissolve 2 tablespoons of sugar in 100ml white wine vinegar, pour over the peppers and tomatoes and cook for a minute or two. Omit the sugar, boiled lemon and coriander.

SWEET AND SOUR MINTY GRILLED COURGETTES

Sweet and sour is one of the tastes the Arabs brought to Sicily in the ninth century. This courgette dish, *zucchine in agrodolce alla menta,* is wonderful with ricotta, which is here as a recommended option.

Serves 4

3 courgettes (about 800g in total)
olive or sunflower oil
100ml white wine vinegar
50g sugar
1 tbsp dried mint
salt and black pepper
extra virgin olive oil, to serve

Preheat the grill to high. Line a baking sheet with foil. Cut each courgette lengthways into 1cm-thick slices. Place them on the foil, brush with oil on both sides and sprinkle lightly with salt. Grill for about 10 minutes, turning them over once, until they are tender and lightly browned in places. Alternatively, you can cook them on a griddle pan.

Heat the vinegar and sugar with the dried mint and some pepper in a small pan over medium heat, stirring until the sugar melts, then simmer for 2 minutes to reduce it a little. Arrange the courgette slices side by side on a serving plate, pour the vinegar dressing over them and add a drizzle of extra virgin olive oil.

Whipped ricotta

Using a fork, whip 250g ricotta with 1½ tablespoons extra virgin olive oil, the grated zest of ½ small lemon, and salt and pepper to taste.

MOZZARELLA SOAKED IN CREAM WITH BABY TOMATOES

In Italy in the 1980s, it was fashionable to call dishes *tricolore* after the green, white and red Italian flag. There was *risotto tricolore* and *pizza tricolore*. The *insalata di mozzarella e pomodori* is still with us because tomatoes and basil are great with mozzarella. In this recipe, very fresh *mozzarella di bufala* is macerated in double cream for a few hours to give a magical 'burrata' effect. Sautéeing the tomatoes gives them a sweet and intense flavour.

Serves 3–6

3 x 125g balls of mozzarella di bufala, each cut into 4 slices

150ml double cream

500g red and yellow baby Santini tomatoes or cherry tomatoes

4 tbsp mild extra virgin olive oil

½ tsp sugar

6 basil sprigs, leaves torn

salt and black pepper

Put the mozzarella in a bowl, cover with the cream and season with salt and pepper. Cover and leave in the fridge for at least 4 hours.

Sauté the baby tomatoes in a pan with 1 tablespoon of the oil for about 8 minutes, adding the sugar and a little salt and pepper, shaking the pan and turning the tomatoes over until they soften and the skins of some of them tear.

Serve the mozzarella at room temperature with the tomatoes on the side. Drizzle with the remaining oil and garnish with the torn basil leaves.

SPELT AND TOMATO SALAD

What is new today is often very old, and what was long seen as poor peasant food is now fashionable. This is true of a group of ancient Mediterranean wheat species known as *farro* in Italy and *épeautre* in France, similar to our spelt. It's a grain on which the Roman armies are said to have marched. This Tuscan salad is charming and satisfying.

Serves 6

250g pearl farro or spelt

200g baby plum tomatoes, halved

½ red onion, finely chopped

6 tbsp extra virgin olive oil

juice of ½–1 lemon, to taste

bunch (25g) of flat-leaf parsley, coarsely chopped

salt and black pepper

Soak the farro or spelt in plenty of cold water for 30 minutes. Rinse, drain and put it in a pan with plenty of water to cover. Bring to the boil and simmer for about 20 minutes or until tender, adding salt towards the end. Drain and put it in a serving bowl.

Add the remaining ingredients and mix well.

Variation

For a simple but delightful Sicilian spelt salad, omit the tomatoes. Instead, mix in 50g raisins (soaked in water for 30 minutes), 50g lightly toasted pine nuts, and the shredded leaves of 3 basil sprigs and 3 mint sprigs.

SHOPPING AT A FARMERS' MARKET IN PROVENCE

The weekly farmers' markets are an important part of the culture and way of life of towns and villages. It is where you meet and socialise and where, visually, the landscape delivers to the table. For me, they are magical.

Going early to choose cheeses and charcuterie, a jam or honey and olives; getting something from an artisan cook and eating it sitting on a bench under a plane tree is my idea of happiness. Then coffee or a glass of iced rosé in a café on the square. After a visit to the butcher and fishmonger, stocking up on fruit and vegetables – fleshy red peppers, heirloom tomatoes, courgettes with their blossoms on, shiny black aubergines, fat garlic heads. Depending on the season, there might be pumpkins, chestnuts, wild mushrooms in large baskets, peaches and apricots, punnets of figs and Muscat grapes. Finally, going away with a couple of local wines, freshly baked bread and bunches of herbs, thinking of what I am going to make…

POTATO SALAD WITH GREEN OLIVE TAPENADE

A Provençal *tapenade aux olives vertes* makes a fantastic dressing for potatoes. Use good-quality pitted olives: I use the large Spanish Queen variety. Serve as a first course alone or as part of a sharing menu.

The French peel the potatoes for their salads and the British do not. I peel them before cooking, but you may prefer to boil them in their skins and peel them when cool enough to handle.

Serves 8

1kg new potatoes, peeled

225g jar (113g drained weight) pitted green olives in brine, drained

7 anchovy fillets in oil, drained

2 tbsp capers, squeezed

1–2 garlic cloves, crushed

1½ tbsp wine vinegar or sherry vinegar

5 tbsp extra virgin olive oil

salt and black pepper, or chilli pepper, to taste

bunch (25g) of flat-leaf parsley, leaves chopped, to serve

Cook the potatoes in boiling salted water until tender right through when you pierce them with a pointed knife.

Put all the remaining ingredients (except the parsley) in a food processor or blender and blend to a thick, rough, oily paste. Taste, and adjust the seasoning if needed.

Drain the potatoes and cut them into quarters or in half if small. Mix with the tapenade until they are well coated and sprinkle with the parsley leaves.

STUFFED PEPPERS WITH BREADCRUMBS, ANCHOVIES, OLIVES AND CAPERS

I have spent years stuffing vegetables in all kinds of ways – with rice, bulgur, meat, cheese. In my family's culture, labouring over food was a way of expressing love for family and honouring guests, and stuffed vegetables was one of those labour-intensive foods. Now, what matters to me is to offer something that delights, and my friends are happier when a dish is quick and easy because they want to make it themselves. These stuffed peppers are quick to make and the stuffing is essentially Mediterranean. Use the long Romano peppers.

Serves 6

3 Romano peppers, cut in half lengthways and seeded

6 anchovy fillets in oil, drained and chopped

6 good-quality black olives, such as Kalamata, pitted and chopped

1 tbsp tiny capers in brine, drained and squeezed

small bunch (15g) of flat-leaf parsley, leaves chopped

40g fresh breadcrumbs

3 tbsp extra virgin olive oil

Preheat the oven to 170°C/150°C fan/gas 3. Line a roasting tin with foil and arrange the peppers cut-side up on the foil. Roast for about 30 minutes until they are soft. Leave to cool.

Mix all the remaining ingredients together to make a stuffing. When the peppers are cool enough to handle, put a little stuffing into each and serve at room temperature.

SPICY ROASTED CARROT SALAD

In Morocco, the appetisers served before a meal are cooked vegetable salads; they often feature carrots, usually flavoured with cumin, which is supposed to stimulate the appetite. The mix of spices in this recipe is particularly delicious. I serve the carrots with labneh (page 45) made with a little salt, flavoured with the grated zest of a lemon.

Serves 6–8

1kg medium carrots, peeled
1½ tsp ground cumin
½ tsp ground coriander
½ tsp ground cinnamon
½ tsp ground ginger
3 garlic cloves, crushed
2–3 tbsp olive oil
1 tbsp honey
juice of ½–1 lemon, to taste
chilli pepper, to taste (optional)
salt and black pepper
2 tbsp extra virgin olive oil, to serve
3 tbsp roughly chopped coriander, to garnish

Preheat the oven to 200°C/180°C fan/gas 6.

Cut the carrots in half, then cut them in half lengthways so that you have wide sticks. Put them in a baking dish.

In a bowl, put the cumin, coriander, cinnamon, ginger, garlic, olive oil, honey, lemon juice, and chilli if using. Season with salt and pepper. Mix very well and pour over the carrots. Turn them with your hands until they are coated all over.

Bake for about 1 hour until the carrots are tender, turning them over once.
Leave to cool.

Serve at room temperature with a drizzle of extra virgin olive oil and a sprinkling of coriander.

AUBERGINES WITH POMEGRANATE DRESSING AND YOGHURT SAUCE

My grandparents moved to Egypt from Syria when the ancient camel caravan trade routes from the East through Aleppo became obsolete (because the building of the Suez canal created a new sea route). They moved into a new quarter that became settled entirely with Syrians. My father, the youngest of eleven and the only boy, was conceived in Syria and born in Cairo. His family always cooked the food of Aleppo. It was part of who we were. This dish, with layers of textures and flavours, is my version of one of the city's delicacies. Serve it as a first course.

Serves 4

olive oil for greasing

2 aubergines (about 300g each), trimmed and cut in half lengthways

1¼ tbsp pomegranate molasses

1¼ tbsp red or white wine vinegar

3 tbsp extra virgin olive oil

salt and black pepper

Yoghurt sauce

200g full-fat natural yoghurt

grated zest of ½ lemon

1–2 tbsp tahini, to taste

1 small garlic clove, crushed (optional)

To garnish

1 tbsp pine nuts

1 tbsp fresh pomegranate seeds

1 tbsp chopped flat-leaf parsley

Preheat the grill to high. Line a baking sheet with foil, brush it with oil and add the aubergines, cut-sides down. Grill for 10–15 minutes until the skins are blistered and the aubergines feel soft inside when you press them – but they should not be too soft. (Alternatively, preheat the oven to 220°C/200°C fan/gas 7, then roast the aubergines for 25–30 minutes.)

When cool enough to handle, use a spoon to scoop out the flesh into a colander and leave for a few minutes for some of the juices to drain.

On a shallow serving dish, cut the aubergine flesh into long strips and then into chunks. Mix the pomegranate molasses, vinegar, oil, salt and pepper, beating well with a fork, and pour over the aubergines. Turn the pieces in the dressing to coat them well.

For the yoghurt sauce, beat the yoghurt with the lemon zest, tahini and garlic, if you like. Spoon it over the aubergines.

Toast the pine nuts in a dry frying pan over medium heat for about 3 minutes, stirring and shaking the pan until light brown spots appear. Keep an eye on them as they burn very quickly. Sprinkle over the dish with the pomegranate seeds and parsley.

AUBERGINES IN A SPICY HONEY SAUCE WITH SOFT GOATS' CHEESE

These are flavours of Morocco that you will encounter in Marseille. Use a delicate scented honey, such as orange blossom or acacia. Make the dish in advance to allow the aubergines to absorb the sauce and serve it at room temperature as a first course or as one of three or four 'sharing' dishes. It's wonderful.

Serves 4–6

4 tbsp olive or sunflower oil

2 aubergines, trimmed and cut into 1cm-thick slices

3 garlic cloves, crushed

¾–1 tbsp grated fresh ginger

3 tbsp lemon juice

4 tbsp honey

large pinch of chilli pepper, or to taste

1 tbsp extra virgin olive oil

300g fresh soft goats' cheese, cut into pieces

1 tbsp chopped flat-leaf parsley

salt

Heat 1½ tablespoons of the olive or sunflower oil in a non-stick sauté pan with a tight lid over medium–high heat, add half of the aubergine slices, sprinkle lightly with salt, and cook covered with the lid for about 15 minutes, turning them over at least once until soft and browned all over. (They fry and steam at the same time.) Remove and set aside, then repeat with another 1½ tablespoons of oil, the remaining aubergine slices and a sprinkling of salt.

Heat the remaining 1 tablespoon of oil together with the garlic in a small frying pan over low heat for moments only, stirring constantly, until the aroma rises and the garlic just begins to colour. Remove from the heat and stir in the ginger, lemon juice, honey, chilli, extra virgin olive oil and a little salt. Mix well and taste to get the balance of sweet and salt right.

Return all the aubergine slices to the sauté pan and pour the honey sauce all over. Cook over low heat for 2–3 minutes, turning the slices to coat them in the sauce. If it seems too dry, add 1–3 tablespoons of water.

Arrange the aubergines on a serving dish with the goats' cheese on the side and sprinkle with the chopped parsley.

CHICKPEAS WITH YOGHURT AND TAHINI SAUCE

Many years ago – during the Lebanese civil war – I received a letter from Beirut, from someone I didn't know. The late Josephine Salam wrote that she had some recipes for me and offered to come to my house and cook them with me. We made so much food that we had to call my neighbours in to help eat it up. After that, we often cooked together, and as she came and went from Lebanon I received an ongoing account of everyday life in her ravaged city. She always managed to put humour into the horror. This elegant version of *fattet hummus* is inspired by her. You can make it with tinned chickpeas but it is the kind of dish that is easy to make in large quantities and, in that case, it is worth making with dried chickpeas.

Serves 4–6

150g chickpeas, soaked overnight in double their volume of water with 1 tsp bicarbonate of soda, or 2 x 400g tins of chickpeas, drained

¼ tsp bicarbonate of soda

400g natural yoghurt, at room temperature

2 tbsp tahini

1–2 garlic cloves, crushed

50g pine nuts

2 tbsp extra virgin olive oil

1 tbsp pomegranate molasses

good pinch of chilli pepper (optional)

1 tbsp chopped flat-leaf parsley

salt, to taste

1 pitta bread, cut open and into triangles, very lightly toasted, to serve

Drain the soaked chickpeas and put them in a pan with plenty of water to cover them by about 1cm and the ¼ teaspoon of bicarbonate of soda (it helps them to soften). Bring to the boil, skim off the foam that forms at the top and simmer, covered, for 20–45 minutes until the chickpeas are soft (the time depends on their type and age). Add water if necessary so that the level remains about 1cm above the chickpeas throughout. When the chickpeas have begun to soften, add some salt.

Mix the yoghurt with the tahini and garlic and add a little salt, to taste.

Toast the pine nuts in a dry frying pan over medium heat for seconds only, stirring, until very lightly browned.

Drain the chickpeas and put them in a wide serving dish, and pour the yoghurt mixture all over them. Drizzle the oil and the pomegranate molasses over the top and, if you like, dust with chilli pepper. Sprinkle with the pine nuts and parsley.

Serve with toasted pitta triangles stuck around the edges.

MASHED CHICKPEAS WITH TURMERIC

Chickpeas with turmeric is peasant food in Tunisia, but it tastes marvellous. With the addition of some Mediterranean store-cupboard specialities, it becomes a glorious, multicoloured party dish.

Serves 6–8

300g dried chickpeas, soaked overnight in double
their volume of water with 1 tsp bicarbonate of soda

½ tsp bicarbonate of soda

5 garlic cloves, peeled

¾–1 tsp ground turmeric

6 tbsp extra virgin olive oil

juice of 1 lemon

salt and black pepper

Optional additions

16 black olives, such as Kalamata

3–4 piquillo peppers in oil, drained and halved

1 boiled lemon (page 226), or preserved lemon, cut into small pieces

1 tbsp drained capers

3 tbsp chopped coriander leaves

Drain the soaked chickpeas and put them in a large pan with about 500ml water – enough to cover them by about 1cm – and the ½ teaspoon of bicarbonate of soda (it helps them to soften). Bring to the boil, skim off the foam that forms at the top, then add the garlic and stir in the turmeric. Simmer, covered, for 20–45 minutes until the chickpeas are very tender (the time depends on their type and age), adding water if necessary to keep them covered. By the end of cooking the liquid should be reduced to a thick sauce. If not, remove the lid and cook uncovered to reduce it.

Keep aside a small handful of chickpeas to use as garnish. Add the oil and lemon juice, salt and pepper to the pan and blend to a rough paste, using a hand blender or food processor.

Spread the paste, hot or cold, in a wide shallow serving platter and garnish with the reserved chickpeas, plus, if you like, one or more of the optional additions.

SPICY BULGUR
AND NUT SALAD

This is a Syrian dish and my family called it *bazargan* because all the ingredients could be bought at the spice bazaar in Aleppo. It is substantial and filling and also amazingly rich and tasty, with a variety of nuts, spices and aromatics. It is easy to make for a lot of people, can be prepared in advance and keeps perfectly well for days. There is also no cooking because bulgur is wheat that has been boiled and dried then 'cracked' – it only needs soaking in boiling water, while all the aromatic ingredients are beaten together as a dressing.

Serve as a first course with Greek-style yoghurt or labneh (page 45). It can be served in a large bowl or elegantly rolled into balls the size of a walnut and cupped in Baby Gem lettuce leaves.

Serves 6

250g bulgur
400ml boiling water, lightly salted
100ml mild extra virgin olive oil
1½ tbsp pomegranate molasses
juice of 2½ lemons
4 tbsp tomato purée
1–1½ tbsp harissa or other hot pepper paste
1½ tsp ground cumin
1 tsp ground coriander
½ tsp ground allspice
100g walnuts, lightly toasted
100g hazelnuts, lightly toasted
50g pistachio nuts, lightly toasted
50g pine nuts, lightly toasted
large bunch (50g) of flat-leaf parsley, leaves chopped
salt, to taste
pomegranate seeds, to garnish (optional)

Put the bulgur in a large bowl and pour the boiling water over it. Leave to soak for 30 minutes until the grains are very tender. Keep turning it over so that the water is absorbed evenly.

For the dressing, beat the oil with the pomegranate molasses and some salt. Add the lemon juice, tomato purée, harissa, cumin, coriander and allspice and beat vigorously with a fork until well blended. Pour over the bulgur and mix very well. Taste and add more salt if necessary.

Coarsely chop the walnuts, hazelnuts and pistachios. Add them to the bulgur, together with the pine nuts and parsley; mix well. If you like, garnish with pomegranate seeds.

YOGHURT AND CUCUMBER SALAD

In this deconstruction of a famous Middle Eastern classic, known more widely by its Greek name *tzatziki*, grated cucumber, dressed with a minty dressing with a touch of orange blossom water, is a topping on creamy yoghurt flavoured with garlic and lemon zest. It is a perfect side to so many dishes in this book – except fish. In Turkey, it is taboo to serve yoghurt with fish, so I don't.

Serves 4

3 small cucumbers or 1 large one

3 tbsp extra virgin olive oil

1 tsp orange blossom water

*grated zest of 1 lemon, plus
2 tbsp lemon juice*

1 mint sprig, leaves finely chopped

200g Greek-style yoghurt

1–2 garlic cloves, crushed

salt

Peel and grate the cucumber and put it in a colander. Sprinkle very generously with salt and mix well, using your hands. Leave to drain for at least 30 minutes.

Whisk together the olive oil, orange blossom water, lemon juice and mint and dress the cucumber with this.

Beat the yoghurt with the lemon zest and garlic. Add a little salt if you like (I don't) and spread on a serving plate. Just before serving, top with the cucumber salad.

STORE-CUPBOARD MEDITERRANEAN SALAD

This is a snack for when people call unexpectedly and stay on. I make it as we sit in the kitchen with a drink. It is inspired by a bar in Barcelona that displayed a huge array of jars and tins and specialised in tapas made entirely from preserves. I've added fresh tomatoes and hard-boiled eggs and serve it with good bread.

Serves 4

4 red piquillo peppers in oil, drained

200g tin tuna, drained

50g tin anchovies, drained

12 black olives

4 ripe plum tomatoes, cut into wedges

*4 hard-boiled eggs,
quartered lengthways*

3 tbsp extra virgin olive oil

1 tbsp white wine vinegar

salt and black pepper

Divide the peppers, tuna, anchovies, olives, tomatoes and eggs between four plates.

Beat the oil and vinegar with salt and pepper and pour a little over each helping.

VEGETABLE SIDES
AND SHARING DISHES

Vegetables have an important place in this part of the world where – until relatively recently – much of the population consisted of impoverished peasants who could rarely afford meat, in some countries maybe only once a week and sometimes only on festive occasions.

The Vaucluse is a department of Provence where I have often stayed with my friend, the late Dutch sculptor Ans Hey, and which is incredibly appealing. Everything is radiant: the luminous sky, its colours fading into pastel tints in the dazzling light; the earth grey and ochre; the houses white or rose or rusty gold; the luxurious vegetation pale, not vivid green. Against it, the different reds of the winter roses and the geraniums and bougainvilleas that come out in the spring are electrifying. The smells are of fig trees or Aleppo pines, or orange and lemon blossom and jasmine and a whole variety of wild herbs basking in the sun. But when I asked farmers how they were, they always replied: 'C'est la catastrophe!' Either the south wind blew just before harvest time and the crops dried out, or they were attacked by frost, or the rains carried away the seed. The reality behind the charm for those living off the land can be one of hardship and constant struggle, where everything is gained by painful effort.

Everywhere in the Mediterranean it is dry with hot summers and mild winters, with rare but violent rainstorms and strong winds. The soil is generally poor and often stony and shallow and only a small part can be cultivated. Crops are at the mercy of the unstable elements. Lands under cultivation are scattered between great stretches of scrub and forest, both on plains and on mountain slopes, and in parts where the desert allows. The olive and the vine are classic types of Mediterranean vegetation that require little moisture. Their long roots, which seek out water deep in the soil, also help them resist the wind's attack. In the past, wheat, maize and barley were important cereal crops that were sometimes rotated with chickpeas, lentils and broad beans. But the grain fields have receded to make way for fruit groves and market gardens and for single-crop cultivation. Although some of the Mediterranean has remained attached to the idea of smallholders growing a variety of crops for the local market, the trend has been for specialised, mass-produced cultivation directed towards the export market.

In an impoverished rural world where the morrow is uncertain, you have to be careful and frugal. Part of the charm of Mediterranean cooking is its sobriety. It is the combination of frugality and fruitfulness, with an abundance of vegetables, grain, pulses, fruit and nuts, that gives it a unique, rustic, healthy quality. Every country has the same vegetables but each has its favourites and each has its special ways of making them a pleasure to eat. When I asked an Italian chef what made the food of the south special, he said a little 'fantasia'. He meant the little personal touches that give real flavour. Around the Mediterranean, these can be the addition of just one herb or a trickle of olive oil to a hot, spicy, peppery sauce.

VEGETABLES POACHED IN STOCK AND WHITE WINE

A usual way with vegetables in the Mediterranean is lightly poached in water and served with a little salt and a dribble of extra virgin olive oil. It is what I cook for myself every day.

For their versions of the vegetable side dish, the nouvelle cuisine chefs of Provence brought tiny baby vegetables into fashion. They poached them briefly in stock, sometimes with a little white wine added, and served them with herbs from their gardens. I adopted this method, and when I have many people for dinner I often serve a large platter with a collection of pretty little vegetables as a first course or side dish. I arrange them pell-mell and dress them with a mild-tasting extra virgin olive oil and a sprinkling of fresh herbs. Everyone loves it.

You can make this in advance and warm it in the oven covered in foil, or serve at room temperature.

Half-fill a large pan with chicken or vegetable stock. Bring to the boil and add salt, 3 or 4 peeled garlic cloves, 4 bay leaves and 2 thyme sprigs. Keeping the stock at a low simmer, add the vegetables in the order in which they need to cook until only just tender. Baby carrots and tiny new potatoes may need about 10 minutes, asparagus 2–3 minutes. Try two, three or four vegetables: baby carrots, tiny new potatoes, baby leeks and artichoke hearts, broad beans, green beans, baby courgettes, cauliflower florets, peas, asparagus spears and Baby Gem lettuces cut in half.

SPRING VEGETABLE MEDLEY

I found this trio of spring vegetables – broad beans, peas and artichokes – cooked together in several countries. I've adopted an Italian version in which they are cooked in a light broth (called *vignole* in Tuscany, *vignarola* in Rome, *frittedda* in Sicily). I make it throughout the year with artichoke hearts in jars and frozen broad beans and petits pois. I eat it with a spoon like a soup and have even served it over pasta as *pasta primavera*. If you have some dry white wine at hand, put some in with the broth. In Spain they add 1–2 tablespoons of brandy. When I use fresh vegetables in spring, I replace the artichokes with asparagus spears.

Serves 4–6

2 tbsp olive oil

1 onion, chopped

250g frozen broad beans, defrosted

4 (8 halves) chargrilled baby artichoke hearts in oil, rinsed

500ml chicken or vegetable stock, or a mix of 200ml dry white wine and 300ml stock

250g petits pois, defrosted

1 tsp sugar (optional)

1 fresh mint sprig, leaves torn

1½ tbsp extra virgin olive oil

salt and black pepper

Warm the olive oil in a sauté pan and fry the onion over medium–low heat, stirring often, for about 8 minutes until soft. Add the broad beans, artichokes and the stock, or wine/stock mixture if using. Stir well and simmer, covered, for 15 minutes.

Stir in the petits pois and cook, covered, for 5 minutes, until all the vegetables are tender. Taste and season with salt and pepper; if you have used dry white wine you might need to add 1 teaspoon of sugar. Stir in the mint and serve with a drizzle of extra virgin olive oil.

ROAST SUMMER VEGETABLES

In Provence, ratatouille is a matter of heated debate – do you fry the vegetables separately, one at a time, or sauté them in the same pan, adding them at different times? Roasting the vegetables is much easier and it intensifies their flavours. Serve them hot or at room temperature, as a side dish or first course, accompanied by slices of toasted bread brushed with extra virgin olive oil. Alternatively, serve hot on a bed of creamy polenta (page 146) or with pasta. The sweet-and-sour variation below makes a good cold appetiser.

Serves 6–8

2 aubergines, trimmed and cut into 3cm chunks

2 courgettes, trimmed and cut into 3cm slices

2 red onions, each cut into 6 wedges

8 small tomatoes

3 thyme or marjoram sprigs, leaves only

6 tbsp olive oil

2 red peppers, seeded and cut into 3cm pieces

2 whole heads of garlic, cloves peeled

salt and black pepper

Preheat the oven to 180°C/160°C fan/gas 4. Line two large baking trays with foil.

Put the aubergines, courgettes, onions and tomatoes on the baking trays and sprinkle with the thyme or marjoram, olive oil and some salt and pepper. Mix well, turning the vegetables over so that they are coated in the oil. Bake for 30 minutes, then take the trays out of the oven.

Turn over the vegetables in the tray that was on the lower oven shelf, add the peppers, and put the tray back in the oven on the higher shelf. Turn over the vegetables in the other tray, add the garlic, and put it on the lower shelf. Roast both trays for a further 15–20 minutes until the vegetables are very soft. If they become brown before they are tender, cover them with foil.

Variations

~ Garnish with one or two of the following: lightly toasted flaked almonds or pine nuts, chopped flat-leaf parsley, garlic croûtons, feta cheese cut into cubes.

~ For a sweet-and-sour version to serve cold: heat 6 tablespoons white or red wine vinegar with 3 tablespoons sugar and stir to dissolve the sugar; sprinkle over the hot vegetables, toss well and leave to cool.

HERBY MASHED POTATOES WITH OLIVE OIL

You will be won over by this Mediterranean counterpart to the mashed potatoes with butter, milk and cream we all love. It makes a wonderful side to many dishes in this book, both hot and cold. I can happily eat it by itself.

Serves 6

750g mashing potatoes, peeled
6 tbsp extra virgin olive oil, or a half-and-half mix of olive and sunflower oil
a handful of chopped flat-leaf parsley
3 spring onions, finely chopped (optional)
salt and black pepper

Boil the potatoes in salted water until soft. Drain, keeping about 150ml of the cooking water.

Mash the potatoes roughly with a potato masher or a fork and beat in the olive oil. Add salt and pepper to taste and a little of the cooking water – enough to give a soft, slightly moist texture. Stir in the parsley and, if you like, the spring onions.

Variation

Instead of parsley, mix in another freshly chopped herb, such as basil, mint, dill or chives.

LEMONY ROAST POTATOES WITH CHERRY TOMATOES AND GARLIC

I love potatoes with lemon. Sweet roasted cherry tomatoes and soft, mildly bitter garlic add complexity to a dish that is delightful hot or cold.

Serves 6

1kg waxy new potatoes
5–6 tbsp olive or sunflower oil
juice of 1½ lemons
300g cherry tomatoes
6 garlic cloves, peeled and cut in half lengthways (optional)
large handful of coriander or dill, coarsely chopped
salt and black pepper

Cook the potatoes, in their skins, in boiling water for about 10 minutes, then drain. Cut them into slices about 1.25cm thick, then put them in a wide baking dish.

Meanwhile, preheat the oven to 240°C/220°C fan/gas 9.

Mix the oil, lemon juice and some salt and pepper, beating with a fork. Pour over the potatoes and use your hands to turn the slices until they are well coated. Add the tomatoes and the garlic, if using.

Roast for 20–30 minutes, turning them once, until the potatoes are crisp and brown. Serve sprinkled with coriander or dill.

ROAST CELERIAC, SWEET POTATO AND CARROT WITH TARRAGON VINAIGRETTE

The sweet aniseed and slightly vanilla flavour of tarragon in the dressing adds an intriguing note to this root vegetable bake. It is a perfect winter accompaniment to meat and poultry grills and roasts and can also be eaten cold as a salad.

Serves 6

1 celeriac
3 sweet potatoes
3 carrots
3 tbsp olive or sunflower oil
salt and black pepper

Tarragon vinaigrette

3 tbsp extra virgin olive oil
1 tbsp vinegar
5 tarragon sprigs, leaves stripped and coarsely chopped

Preheat the oven to 200°C/180°C fan/gas 6. Line a large roasting tin with foil.

Peel the celeriac, sweet potatoes and carrots and cut them into chunks of about 3cm. Put them in the roasting tin, sprinkle with salt and pepper and pour over the olive or sunflower oil. Use your hands to turn the vegetables until they are well coated.

Roast for 50–60 minutes, turning them once, until they are tender and lightly browned in places. Cover with foil if they are getting too brown towards the end of the cooking time.

For the vinaigrette, mix the oil, vinegar, and salt and pepper to taste, beating with a fork, then stir in the tarragon. Pour over the roasted vegetables, turning them so that they are well coated.

FRITTATA WITH CHEESE AND HERBS

This is a Slovenian *frtalja*. When I was a child, my nanny, Maria Koron, was a Slovene from a village called Batuje in a part of Slovenia that had been taken by Italy during the First World War. She talked to us in Italian and cooked for us when we were small. A few years ago, I was contacted by Barbara Skubic, who was part of an organisation of women who were finding out about their mothers' and grandmothers' lives in Egypt. They found me through a cake Maria made called *potica* that appeared in one of my books. In her first letter, Barbara had a list of questions about Maria. The last one was 'Did you love her?' I replied 'We adored her!' I was invited to take part in a festival of Egypt in Ljubljana. I got to meet Maria's family and to visit her village. I learned that she had been a novice nun, something she never told us, but was convinced by her family to go to work in Egypt and send money home, as was usual in Slovenia at the time. I brought back to London her family's own salamis, cheeses, wines and *potica*.

I vary the herbs, depending on what I have to hand, from parsley or tarragon alone to a mix of two or three, such as chives, dill, basil, mint. Use scissors to snip chives into small pieces, or basil leaves into larger ones.

Accompanied by soured cream or yoghurt and a salad, this makes a light meal.

Serves 2

40g plain flour
100ml whole milk
4 large eggs
100g mature Cheddar, grated
bunch of fresh herbs, snipped with scissors
15g butter
salt and black pepper

Put the flour in a bowl and gradually add the milk, beating vigorously with a fork, then beat in the eggs to make a batter.

Add the cheese, some salt and pepper, and the herbs – there should be plenty of herbs and the frittata should be quite green.

Heat the butter in a non-stick frying pan. Swirl it around until it sizzles, then pour in the batter and cook over low heat for about 8 minutes or until the bottom and sides are set.

Meanwhile, preheat the grill to hot.

Put the pan under the grill for a moment only to set the top. It should still be creamy. Serve hot.

POTATO OMELETTE

This comforting omelette should be *really* creamy inside. For an Italian *frittata di patate alle erbe*, serve with the herb dressing below. For a Tunisian version, serve with the spicy tomato sauce below.

Serves 4–6

300g potatoes, peeled and cut into similar-sized pieces

2 onions, halved and sliced

4 tbsp olive oil

6 large eggs

salt and black pepper

Boil the potatoes for about 15 minutes until tender, then drain and mash them roughly.

Fry the onions in 2 tablespoons of the oil in a non-stick frying pan over low heat for about 15 minutes until soft, stirring often, then turn up the heat to medium–high and stir constantly until golden.

Beat the eggs with a fork. When the potatoes and onions have cooled a little, add them to the eggs and mix well. Season to taste with salt and pepper.

Preheat the grill to very hot. Wipe the frying pan with kitchen paper and heat the remaining oil. Pour in the egg, onion and potato mixture and cook over medium–low heat for 3–4 minutes or until the bottom is set and lightly browned, shaking the pan to make sure that the omelette does not stick. Then put it under the grill for about 2 minutes until the top is dry and slightly springy to the touch. The omelette should be creamy – it is fine if it is still a little liquid inside.

Serve warm or at room temperature.

Variations

~ For an Italian herb dressing: mix 2 tablespoons lemon juice with 6 tablespoons extra virgin olive oil, 2 tablespoons chopped fresh tarragon, 1 teaspoon grated orange zest and some salt and pepper.

~ For a Tunisian tomato 'jam': put 400g tinned chopped tomatoes in a frying pan and stir in 1 tablespoon runny honey and 1 tablespoon rose water. Cook over medium heat for 10 minutes until thick and jammy. Season to taste with a little salt and plenty of chilli and cook for 2 minutes more. Serve warm or at room temperature.

TARTE PISSALADIÈRE

I find the combination of anchovy fillets with meltingly soft onions irresistible. The *pissaladière* is at the heart of the cuisine of Nice, but in Nice they tell you it was born in neighbouring Liguria. I was in Nice with Alan Davidson when we were booked to entertain the wives at an international frozen food conference with stories about food. In the end we entertained the husbands, too. Mary Bloom, an American journalist at the *International Herald Tribune* who was writing a humorous piece about the event, invited us to dinner at the great Jacques Maximin's Chantecler at the Negresco. It was a fantastic Mediterranean *menu dégustation* by one of the first innovative chefs and the *pissaladière* was on a shortcrust base instead of the usual yeast dough.

Serves 6

Shortcrust pastry

125g unsalted butter
250g plain flour
¼ tsp salt
1 egg, separated
1–2 tbsp milk, if necessary

Filling

3 tbsp olive oil
4 large onions (about 800g), halved and sliced
16 anchovy fillets in oil, drained
6 pitted black olives, halved
salt and black pepper

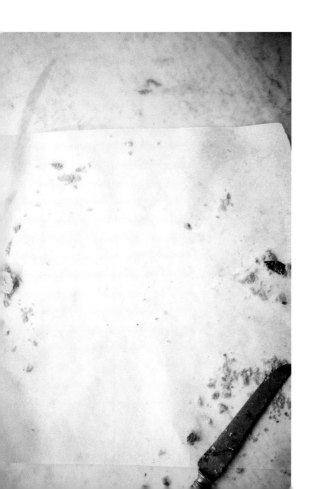

For the pastry, cut the butter into small pieces and rub it into the flour and salt until the texture is like damp sand. Add the egg yolk, mix well, and work very briefly with your hand until the dough holds together in a soft ball, adding a little milk if necessary. Wrap in clingfilm or greaseproof paper and leave in a cool place for 1 hour.

For the filling, heat the oil in a large sauté pan with a lid. Put in the onions and cook, covered, over very low heat, stirring often, for about 55–60 minutes until they are meltingly soft, almost a purée but not at all coloured (if they start to turn brown before they are soft, add 2–3 tablespoons of water). Add salt and pepper and cook uncovered to let any liquid evaporate.

Preheat the oven to 200°C/180°C fan/gas 6. Grease a 28cm shallow tart tin with a removable bottom and line with the pastry, pressing it in with the palm of your hand (with this soft buttery dough, it is easier to do this than to roll it out) and pressing it up the sides of the tin. Prick the bottom in a few places with a fork and brush with the egg white. Bake for 10 minutes.

Spread the onions over the pastry, arrange the anchovy fillets in a lattice pattern on top, and press the olives into the onions in between the lattice. Bake for about 20 minutes.

Serve hot or warm, cut into wedges.

POTATOES, ASPARAGUS TIPS AND EGGS

My daughter Anna and her three daughters, Sarah, Ruby and Nelly, asked for recipes of the dishes I have cooked for them since I started this book. They became passionate cooks and my most important testers, with Anna making meticulous notes and suggestions. This simple bake has become one of their regular snack meals.

Serves 4

500g new potatoes, peeled
200g asparagus tips
4–5 tbsp olive oil
4 large eggs
25g butter
salt and black pepper

Cook the potatoes in boiling water until they are tender.

Meanwhile, preheat the oven to 200°C/180°C fan/gas 6.

When cooked, slice the potatoes into a baking dish. Add the asparagus tips, sprinkle with salt and a little pepper and drizzle with the olive oil. Turn the vegetables until they are evenly coated.

Bake until the asparagus is tender, 15–20 minutes depending on how thick the asparagus tips are.

In a large frying pan, fry the eggs in the butter, sprinkle with salt and serve on top of the vegetables. The yolks should be still runny.

WITH GRAIN

The entire Mediterranean region lives from agriculture. The soil and the climate are ideal for growing old-world vegetables, as well as those arrived from the Americas in the sixteenth century, and grain. Wheat was part of the famous triad, with grapes and olives, that the Greeks and Romans planted throughout the ancient world, and is eaten today as pasta, bulgur and couscous. Barley is indigenous to the region, rice was introduced by the Arabs, and maize came from the Americas.

At an empty café in the Piazza del Campo in Siena, an old man sat alone at the next table. I smiled. Pointing to a chair, he said: 'Join me.' Telling him I was researching the local food and could I ask him about it, I took out my pad and started: What region are you from? What did your parents and grandparents do? What are your favourite dishes? He did not expect that but was happy to chat. His was a family of ten. They had been peasant farmers on an estate in Tuscany. They had cultivated the land and given half the produce to the landlord as rent. They had grown wheat, vegetables and fruit, had olive trees, kept pigs, rabbits and hens, and made wine, olive oil and salami. They ate what they grew – tomatoes, pumpkins, artichokes, spinach, courgettes, other things, too – and pasta. There was a herb, usually sage or rosemary. The family no longer farmed. Giuseppe was helping to organise the Palio, the horse race between the city *contrade* (neighbourhoods). His favourite dish was chicken with grapes.

In Italy, in the 1980s, I was hearing so many similar stories. Country life had changed dramatically in the 1960s when the system of share cropping was abolished. People left the land to work in factories, and landowners sold their estates to entrepreneurs who started intensive farming with tractors and machinery. The old agriculture of intermingled vines, mulberry and olive trees on the hill slopes, with little patches of wheat, maize and pulses, where large families of tenants had spent their days fighting their way through the entanglements to pick everything by hand, was replaced by a single-crop industrial agriculture.

But the dishes that were born in the old life never disappeared and are now very popular. Every generation has a way of pulling out from tradition what fits their ideology and what they love. We too love rustic food. On a week-long gastronomic visit to Puglia with a group of American chefs and food writers, we were sometimes given a choice of menu by the hosts. The group always said they wanted *cucina povera* (poor food), which was trending in America. We were given the local national dish of *fave e cicoria*, a purée of cooked mashed dried broad beans with bitter leaves that was sometimes served as a soup and sometimes as a pasta.

Dishes that combine grain and vegetables are ideal vegetarian fare, substantial enough to serve as a main dish, easy to partner with other dishes, and also perfect, in a small portion, as a first course before meat or fish. They are born of the land and linked to an old rural way of life. That is why they have powerful nostalgic appeal.

VEGETABLE COUSCOUS

This looks complex, with lots of ingredients, but is really easy. I make it when I have invited a lot of people and I know some of them are vegetarian. Instead of cooking the vegetables in the broth, I roast them so they keep their individual flavours, and I enrich the broth with herbs and spices. I prepare it all in advance – the grain in a huge terracotta dish that can go from the oven to the table – and reheat just before serving. I usually also serve the tomato 'jam' on page 155 alongside.

Serves 8

3 aubergines, trimmed and cut into 4cm chunks

2 red peppers, seeded and cut into 4cm pieces

400g squash, cut into slices or cubes

1 celeriac, peeled and cut into 3cm chunks

2 carrots, peeled and cut into 3cm slices

olive oil

500g couscous

salt and black pepper

Broth

1 large onion, chopped

2 tbsp olive oil

3 garlic cloves, chopped

1 large tomato, skinned and chopped

1.25 litres vegetable stock (use 2 stockpots or stock cubes)

1 cinnamon stick

¼ tsp ground allspice

½ tsp ground ginger

good pinch of saffron threads or 1 tsp ground turmeric

400g tin chickpeas, drained and rinsed (optional)

large bunch (50g) of coriander, leaves chopped

bunch (25g) of flat-leaf parsley, leaves chopped

Peppery sauce

1–2 tbsp harissa, or to taste

Preheat the oven to 180°C/160°C fan/gas 4. Arrange the vegetables in one or two foil-lined roasting tins, sprinkle with salt and drizzle about 5 tablespoons of olive oil over them, tossing the vegetables to coat them all over. Roast for 45 minutes or until the vegetables are very soft, turning them over once.

Put the couscous into a large baking dish you can serve it in. Add ½–1 teaspoon of salt to 600ml warm water (half boiling, half cold) and gradually pour this all over the couscous, stirring so that it is absorbed evenly. Leave to swell for 10 minutes. Now, here is the secret for fluffy couscous: stir in 2 tablespoons of olive oil and rub the couscous between your hands above the dish to aerate the grains and break up any lumps.

For the broth, fry the onion in the oil, stirring over low heat until soft. Add the garlic and stir for a few seconds, until the aroma rises, then add the tomato and cook, stirring, for 3 minutes. Pour in the stock and add the cinnamon stick, allspice, ginger, saffron or turmeric and the chickpeas, if using. Bring to the boil, add salt and pepper and simmer over low heat for 10 minutes.

If you've made everything in advance, you'll need to reheat 15 minutes before you are ready to serve. Preheat the oven to 180°C/160°C fan/gas 4. Cover the dish of couscous with foil and put it in the oven, and put the vegetables on the shelf underneath. Bring the broth to the boil, take off the heat and stir in the chopped coriander and parsley.

To make a hot peppery sauce to pass round, put 2 ladlefuls of the hot broth in a bowl or jug and mix in the harissa to taste.

To serve, fluff up the steaming hot couscous with a fork, breaking up any lumps. Ladle some of the broth over the couscous, enough to moisten, but not so much that it is swimming in broth. Serve the rest on the side for guests to help themselves to more as they wish. Serve it in bowls or soup plates with the vegetables on top, and pass round the peppery harissa sauce for everyone to help themselves.

CREAMY POLENTA WITH MUSHROOMS

One magical night on the terrace overlooking the canal at the Gritti Palace in Venice I attended a banquet for chefs from all over Italy. The menu represented traditional dishes from all the regions. The local offering was wild mushrooms on creamy polenta. The wild mushrooms were magnificent – I had seen basketfuls at the Rialto market earlier, and the polenta was ever so light and creamy. Shiitake and chestnut mushrooms are also lovely cooked this way.

Serves 4

750g mushrooms

4 tbsp extra virgin olive oil

2 garlic cloves, peeled

3 tbsp dry white wine (if you have an open bottle)

100ml chicken or vegetable stock

2 tbsp chopped flat-leaf parsley

salt and black pepper

Creamy polenta

1 litre whole milk or water

½ tsp salt

165g instant polenta

20g butter

50g Parmesan or Grana Padano, grated

Clean off any dirt from the mushrooms and trim the base of the stalks if necessary. Leave them whole or cut large ones in half.

Heat the oil and garlic in a large sauté pan. Put in the mushrooms and cook quickly over high heat for 2 minutes, turning them over with a spatula and adding salt and pepper. They will absorb the oil and release their liquid. When it evaporates, add the wine, if using, and the stock and cook over medium heat for about 4 minutes until the liquid is reduced a little. Remove the garlic and add the parsley.

For the polenta, pour the milk or water into a large pan, add the salt and bring to the boil. Take the pan off the heat and pour in the polenta in a thin stream, whisking vigorously, then continue to cook over low heat, stirring continuously with the whisk or a wooden spoon for 2 minutes to avoid lumps forming. Cover the pan and cook over very low heat for another 8 minutes. It will gurgle and splatter. Then stir in the butter and the cheese.

Serve the polenta with the mushrooms on top.

Variations

~ For a stronger mushroom flavour, pour 250ml boiling water over 40g dried porcini and leave to soak for 30 minutes. Pour off most of the soaking water – leaving behind any grit – and use instead of the stock. Add the drained porcini to the fresh mushrooms.

~ If you want to make the polenta in advance, pour it into a well-oiled baking dish to a thickness of about 2cm; reheat in the oven, preheated to 200°C/180°C fan/gas 6.

~ For grilled polenta, make the polenta in advance and pour into a well-oiled baking dish to a thickness of about 2cm. Let it cool and then cut it into four slices. Brush them lightly with oil and toast under the grill until lightly browned on both sides.

SPINACH, RAISINS, PINE NUTS AND CRÈME FRAÎCHE WITH POLENTA

I have eaten many lovely spinach dishes, but the Catalan one with raisins and pine nuts with added crème fraîche is my favourite. I serve it on polenta or on green tagliatelle.

Serves 4

320g spinach
150ml crème fraîche
2 tbsp pine nuts, lightly toasted
2 tbsp raisins, soaked in water for 20 minutes
salt and black pepper

Wash the spinach and, if necessary, remove any thick, tough stems. Drain well. Press the leaves into a big pan. Put the lid on tightly and cook over medium–high heat for moments only, until they crumple into a soft mass. They will steam in the water that clings to them. If the spinach is young and ready-washed, put 3–4 tablespoons of water in the pan with the leaves to create the steam.

Pour out any liquid, stir in the crème fraîche, season with salt and pepper, and add the pine nuts and raisins. Stir gently and heat through.

Serve on creamy or grilled polenta, following the instructions on pages 146–7.

Pictured on page 147.

BARLEY WITH MUSHROOMS AND CHESTNUTS

This is a heartwarming rural winter dish with a grand finishing touch. You can use pot barley instead of pearl barley: pot barley is more nutritious but takes longer to cook and does not result in a creamy dish. The instructions on my supermarket packet of pearl barley say it takes 45–60 minutes, but if you soak it overnight the cooking time is reduced to about 30 minutes. Check the packet instructions for soaking and cooking the grain.

Serves 4

165g pearl barley, soaked in plenty of water overnight

750ml water

2 chicken or vegetable stockpots or stock cubes

400g chestnut mushrooms, quartered

3 tbsp sunflower or olive oil

2 garlic cloves, crushed

180g pack cooked whole chestnuts

2–3 tbsp ruby port

25g butter, cut into pieces

3 tbsp double cream

2 tbsp chopped flat-leaf parsley (optional)

salt and black pepper

Drain the barley and put it in a pan with the water and the stockpots or stock cubes. Add some salt, bring to the boil, cover and simmer over low heat until the grain is tender. Keep checking until the grain is as soft and chewy as you like it. It should be moist with a little liquid. Add a little water if it gets too dry and drain it if there is too much liquid. (If you let it sit, the grain will absorb any remaining liquid and become softer.)

Meanwhile, sauté the mushrooms in the oil in a large frying pan with a lid on, turning them over once and shaking the pan, until they release their juices. Remove the lid and let the juices evaporate, then add the garlic and some salt and pepper, and cook, stirring, for a minute or two over high heat. Add the chestnuts and port and cook for 2 minutes more.

You can do all this in advance. Just before you are ready to serve, reheat the barley, adding a little water if necessary, and the mushroom and chestnut mixture. Mix them together, then stir in the butter and the cream. Serve sprinkled with parsley if you like.

Note

There are some who would serve this with grated Parmesan, but for me it is so good as it is.

GREEN BARLEY 'RISOTTO' WITH PEAS AND ASPARAGUS

Although this is called risotto, it is treated differently from a real risotto made with rice. It is easier to cook because you do not need to keep stirring while adding the wine and stock, and there is no risk of overcooking. I often make double the quantity. When my granddaughter Ruby made it for a party with her friends at university she had one complaint: 'There was not enough. Everyone wanted more.'

You can make this in advance and heat it through before serving, but cook the asparagus at the last minute. The instructions on my packet of barley say it takes 45–60 minutes, but it only takes about 30 minutes if the grain is soaked overnight. If you do soak it overnight, it will need less water – perhaps 400ml.

Serves 4

180g pearl barley

1 onion, chopped

2 tbsp olive oil

500ml water, plus 100ml more if needed

200ml dry white wine

2 chicken or vegetable stockpots or stock cubes

200g frozen petits pois

4–5 tbsp crème fraîche

grated zest of ½ lemon

200g asparagus tips, trimmed and cut into pieces

salt and black pepper

1 lemon, quartered, to serve

grated Parmesan or Grana Padano, to serve

Wash the barley in a bowl of cold water and rinse in a sieve under cold running water.

Fry the onion in the oil in a large pan over low heat, stirring often, for 5–8 minutes until it is soft but not coloured.

Pour in 500ml of water and the wine, add the stockpots or stock cubes and bring to the boil. Pour in the barley, cover, and simmer over low heat until the grain is tender, adding salt and pepper midway during the cooking. It can take from 30 to 60 minutes, depending on the grain, if it was soaked overnight, and on how soft you like it. Add water if it is dry. It should be very moist with a little liquid. (If you let it sit, the grain will absorb any remaining liquid and become softer.)

Cook the petits pois for 5 minutes in a little boiling water, then drain, keeping the cooking water. Using a hand blender, blend to a rough purée, adding about 5 tablespoons of the cooking water.

You can do all this in advance. Just before you are ready to serve, reheat the barley, adding a little water if needed. Reheat the pea purée and stir it into the barley with the crème fraîche and lemon zest.

While the barley is reheating, poach the asparagus pieces in salted water for 2 minutes, or until they are al dente, then drain. Serve the barley with the asparagus on top. Pass round the lemon quarters and the grated cheese.

SPICED SAFFRON RICE

Since Roman times, Arabs were engaged as middlemen in the transport of spices and aromatics to Europe from the East. Each country on the route adopted favourites that have endured. You can serve this festive Arabian rice as a side with many dishes, and you must try the pumpkin or butternut squash variation below. It is the kind of dish I could imagine garnished with gold leaf in Renaissance Italy – something that is back in fashion today.

Serves 6–8

500g basmati rice

900ml chicken or vegetable stock (use 2 stockpots or stock cubes) or water

½ tsp ground cardamom or 12 cardamom pods, cracked

6 cloves

3 cinnamon sticks

½ tsp saffron threads or 1 tsp ground turmeric

75g butter, cut into pieces, or 3 tbsp sunflower oil

salt and black pepper

Some basmati rice needs rinsing under cold water (check the packet instructions).

In a pan, bring the stock to the boil with the ground cardamom or cracked pods, cloves and cinnamon sticks, and simmer for 10 minutes.

Add the saffron or turmeric and a little salt and pepper and pour in the rice. Let it come back to the boil, stir well, then lower the heat to a minimum and cook over low heat, with the lid on, for about 20 minutes, until little holes appear on the surface and the rice is tender.

Stir in the butter or oil. Serve the rice hot, in a mound.

Pumpkin or butternut squash pilaf

I buy butternut squash already peeled at the supermarket for this. Preheat the oven to 200°C/180°C fan/gas 6. Cut 750g pumpkin or butternut squash into 2cm cubes. Put it in a baking dish, season with salt and pepper, add 3–4 tablespoons oil and turn the pieces to coat them all over, then bake for 40–45 minutes, turning them over once, until very tender and beginning to caramelise. Cover with foil if they are becoming too brown towards the end. Stir into the rice.

TURMERIC RICE WITH SPINACH AND YOGHURT SAUCE

We thought our aunt Regine was the most beautiful woman in Cairo. She loved beautiful things and delicate flavours. One of her recipes was a spinach and yoghurt soup with rice and turmeric. I have turned it into a colourful and aromatic rice dish.

Serves 6

300g long grain or basmati rice

1 litre chicken or vegetable stock (or water with 1 stockpot or stock cube)

1¼ tsp ground turmeric

400g young spinach leaves, rinsed if necessary

7 tbsp extra virgin olive oil

juice of 1 lemon

salt and black pepper

Yoghurt sauce

500g natural yoghurt

1–2 garlic cloves, crushed

grated zest of 1 lemon

Some basmati rice needs rinsing under cold water (check the packet instructions).

Bring the stock to the boil in a pan with the turmeric and some salt. Pour in the rice, stir well, cover and cook over medium heat for about 10–15 minutes (it varies depending on the type and quality of the rice so check the packet instructions) until it is only just tender. Don't let it get too soft. Add a little water if it becomes too dry before it is cooked, or strain if there is a lot of liquid left. Pour into a wide serving dish.

While the rice is cooking, put the spinach leaves in a large pan. If you have rinsed them, they only need the water that clings to them. If they are dry, add 4–5 tablespoons water. Put the lid on and cook over high heat for moments only, until the leaves crumple into a soft mass. Lift them out, leaving any liquid behind, and add them to the rice.

Mix well and dress with a mixture of extra virgin olive oil, lemon juice, salt and pepper.

For the yoghurt sauce, beat the yoghurt with the garlic and lemon zest. Serve it on the side.

HERBED RICE WITH TOMATO 'JAM'

Here, the rice is simply boiled, and just as it is about to be drained, a large amount of chopped fresh herbs are stirred in: they cling to the rice and stay very green and fresh. Choose two or more herbs, from parsley, mint, chives and dill.

This tomato sauce is inspired by a Moroccan relish, a *confiture* or 'jam', so-called because it is thick and dense, sweet and aromatic with honey and rose water, with chilli to mitigate the sweetness. I always make too much and keep any left over in the fridge to use with other dishes.

Serves 4

250g basmati or long grain rice
large bunch (75g) of herbs, leaves chopped
3 tbsp extra virgin olive oil
salt, to taste

Tomato 'jam'

2 tbsp olive or sunflower oil
3 garlic cloves, crushed
2 x 400g tins chopped tomatoes
2 tbsp runny honey
2 tbsp rose water (optional)
chilli pepper, to taste

Some basmati rice needs rinsing under cold water (check the packet instructions).

Make the tomato 'jam' first. In a wide sauté pan or frying pan, warm the oil over low heat, add the garlic and cook for a few seconds, stirring until the aroma rises and it just begins to colour. Take the pan off the heat and pour in the chopped tomatoes, then simmer, uncovered, over medium heat for about 25 minutes until thick and jammy.

Stir in the honey and rose water, some salt and chilli to taste, and cook for 5 minutes over low heat. Pour into a bowl to pass around or serve on the side with the rice.

Cook the rice in plenty of boiling salted water for 10–15 minutes, stirring once, until tender (check the packet instructions). Throw in the herbs, stir and drain at once. Taste for salt and stir in the extra virgin olive oil.

LENTILS AND RICE WITH DATES AND CARAMELISED ONIONS

When my parents settled in London, my mother, missing her family, her friends and her old life, threw herself into cooking. In Egypt she had left it to the cook; in London it was a passion. To please my father, she cooked the remembered dishes of his childhood. This is the Egyptian *megadarra* he loved – with added dates.

The lentils you get in supermarkets do not need soaking and take no more than 20 minutes to cook, so you can cook them together with the rice, but check the packet instructions, especially for the rice, as cooking times can vary. This is traditionally a first course to be eaten at room temperature, but with the optional accompaniments it is the star of a vegetarian Middle Eastern meal.

Serves 4–6

2 large onions, halved and thickly sliced

6 tbsp olive oil

180g brown or green lentils, rinsed

200g basmati rice, rinsed

1 tsp ground cinnamon

¼ tsp ground allspice

12 pitted soft dried dates such as Medjool, coarsely chopped

salt and black pepper

Accompaniments (optional)

250g halloumi cheese, cut into 8 slices

1 lemon, cut into wedges

Labneh (page 45) or 450g Greek-style yoghurt mixed with salt and 1 crushed garlic clove

Spicy tomato 'jam' (page 155)

Cucumber and tomato salad (page 84)

In a wide frying pan, fry the onions in 2 tablespoons of the oil, stirring often. Start over low heat, with the lid on, and when the onions are very soft continue over medium heat until they are really dark brown – not black or burned – about 25 minutes.

Bring about 1.8 litres of water to the boil and throw in the lentils. Simmer for 10 minutes, add salt, then throw in the rice, add the cinnamon and allspice, and cook for 10–15 minutes until the rice and lentils are tender.

Drain and pour into a wide serving dish. Add salt to taste (it needs a lot) and pepper, the dates and the remaining oil. Mix very gently, turning over with a spatula, so as not to break the grains of rice. Serve warm or at room temperature, with the caramelised onions sprinkled over.

Serve, if you like, with any or all of the optional accompaniments. Cook the halloumi slices on an oiled griddle pan or non-stick frying pan over medium–high heat until browned on both sides. Do this just before serving so that the cheese is still very hot and soft, as it becomes rubbery when it cools.

BULGUR PILAF WITH CHICKPEAS, AUBERGINES AND TOMATOES

This rich Levantine combination is immensely satisfying, with layers of flavour and aroma. The optional halloumi cheese makes it a meal in itself. Accompany if you like with Greek yoghurt and cucumber and tomato salad (page 84). As with anything cooked with oil, leftovers can be eaten cold – but not, in this case, if there is halloumi, as it becomes rubbery when cold.

Serves 6–8

5 tbsp olive oil

2 aubergines, trimmed and cut into 3cm cubes

300g cherry or Santini tomatoes

2 onions, chopped

3 garlic cloves, chopped

350g bulgur

400g tin chickpeas, drained and rinsed

1½–2 tbsp tomato purée

1 tsp ground cinnamon

½ tsp ground allspice

1 tsp ground cumin

good pinch of chilli pepper

500ml boiling water

2 x 250g packs halloumi cheese (optional)

3 tbsp extra virgin olive oil

salt and black pepper

Heat 3 tablespoons of the oil in a sauté pan with a tight-fitting lid and put in the aubergines. Cook over medium heat, turning the cubes over with a spatula so that all have a few minutes to get browned, add salt and pepper and put the lid back on so that they steam in their own juice for about 15 minutes. Put in the cherry tomatoes, turn them over with the aubergines, then continue to cook, covered, for about 8 minutes, until they are soft and begin to release some juice.

In a large pan, fry the onions in the remaining oil over medium heat for 8 minutes, stirring often, until soft and beginning to colour. Add the garlic and cook, stirring, for 2 minutes or until the aroma rises and it begins to colour. Take off the heat and stir in the bulgur and chickpeas.

Put the tomato purée into a measuring jug and add the cinnamon, allspice, cumin, chilli pepper and some salt. Pour in the boiling water and stir vigorously, then pour this into the pan with the bulgur and mix well. Bring to the boil, cover, and cook over low heat for 15 minutes. Taste for salt: you will probably need more.

If adding halloumi, cut the cheese into 3cm cubes and cook quickly over medium–high heat in a non-stick frying pan with a tiny amount of oil, turning the pieces to brown them all over. Mix into the bulgur.

Turn the bulgur into a large baking dish and mix in the aubergines and tomatoes. Serve with the extra virgin olive oil drizzled over.

Note

To reheat before serving, cover with foil and warm through for 10–15 minutes in an oven preheated to 200°C/180°C fan/gas 6.

TAGLIOLINI WITH LEMON

Many Italian dishes have a squeeze of lemon or a hint of its zest, but in these incredibly delicious Sicilian *tagliolini al limone*, lemon is the star. Everybody loves this. Serve as a first course.

Serves 2–4

200g tagliolini
salt
grated zest and juice of 1 lemon
6 tbsp (90ml) double cream
salt and black pepper
grated Parmesan or Grana Padano, to serve

Cook the tagliolini in boiling salted water according to the packet instructions.

In a serving bowl, mix the lemon zest and juice with the cream and add salt to taste.

When the pasta is cooked al dente, drain and mix with the sauce.

Let everyone help themselves to pepper and grated Parmesan.

MALLOREDDUS AL CAPRINO FRESCO

At a hunting lodge in Sardinia I was the only other person in the dining room when a large group of hunters – all men who were singing loudly – invited me to join them at their table. The manageress promptly told me to go back to my own table and to leave the next day. She had already chased me out of the kitchen that morning, even though I showed her a letter from a newspaper saying I was writing a piece for them. The cooks were making *malloreddus,* the conch-shaped ridged Sardinian pasta, with caprino cheese for their own meal. It is delicious but very rich; I serve a small amount for a first course. You can use ridged penne instead, because they too will hold the creamy sauce well. Saffron, another product of Sardinia, is optional.

Serves 4

200g malloreddus or ridged penne
250g fresh soft goats' cheese
grated zest of ½ lemon
grated zest of ½ orange
pinch of saffron threads (optional)
salt and black pepper

Cook the pasta in boiling salted water according to the packet instructions.

Mash the cheese with a fork in a wide pan. Add the grated zests, salt and pepper and 1 or 2 tablespoons of the boiling pasta water. If using saffron, put it in a small bowl or cup and add 2 tablespoons of the boiling pasta water; let it infuse for 2–3 minutes, then add it to the cheese. Stir vigorously to make a creamy sauce. Heat gently when the pasta is ready.

When the pasta is cooked al dente, drain, reserving a few tablespoons of the cooking water. Transfer to the pan with the cheese, mix well, adding 1–2 tablespoons of the cooking water so that the sauce is creamy. Serve hot.

SPAGHETTI WITH GARLIC, OIL AND CHILLI

I have a special fondness for this simple dish because I first tasted it when I was a student at Saint Martin's School of Art in London and the sculptor Eduardo Paolozzi invited a few of us to eat it at his studio. We were enthralled. Many years later, when I spent time in the kitchen of a hotel in Sicily that specialised in wedding parties, the tired chefs – at the end of their day preparing extraordinarily rich banquets – sat together and ate *pasta aglio, olio e peperoncino*.

Serves 4–6

400g spaghetti
5 garlic cloves, finely chopped
2 fresh chillies, seeded and finely chopped
100ml extra virgin olive oil
bunch (25g) of flat-leaf parsley, leaves chopped
salt

Start cooking the pasta in plenty of boiling salted water according to the packet instructions, and begin the sauce. Heat the garlic and chillies in 2–3 tablespoons of the oil, stirring until the aroma rises and the garlic only just begins to colour. Remove from the heat and add the remaining oil.

When the pasta is cooked al dente, drain and transfer to the pan with the sauce. Toss thoroughly, adding salt and a generous sprinkling of parsley.

Variation

Other herbs, such as basil and mint, are sometimes added with the parsley. A chef in Trapani, in Sicily, said he used thirteen, including marjoram, oregano, thyme, sage and rosemary, and called it *spaghetti alle erbe*. I didn't believe him. However, you might like to add a few.

SPAGHETTI WITH ANCHOVIES AND OLIVES

In Naples and Sicily, they have an aristocratic *cucina nobile*, but it is their *cucina povera* (povera means 'poor') that has the richest flavours. These *spaghetti poveri* are for anchovy lovers like me. I often make it for myself and have all the ingredients at hand in the cupboard. Use good-tasting olives, such as Italian Taggiasche or Greek Kalamata.

Serves 3

250g spaghetti

4–5 garlic cloves, chopped

6 tbsp extra virgin olive oil

½–1 fresh hot red chilli, seeded and finely chopped,
or a good pinch of chilli pepper or flakes

60g anchovy fillets in oil from a jar, drained and chopped

100g pitted black olives, cut into pieces

bunch (25g) of flat-leaf parsley, leaves chopped

salt

Get all the ingredients chopped and ready before putting the spaghetti into boiling salted water to cook according to the packet instructions.

In a wide frying pan, heat the garlic in 2 tablespoons of the oil over low heat for a few seconds, until the aroma rises. Add the chilli and anchovies and cook, stirring until the anchovies 'melt' into the oil. Take off the heat and add the olives and parsley.

When the pasta is cooked al dente, drain and transfer to the pan with the sauce. Add the remaining oil and mix very well.

PASTA WITH FRESH TOMATOES, GARLIC AND BASIL

A British magazine had arranged for me to telephone Italian celebrities and ask them for their favourite pasta recipe. Luciano Pavarotti was in a hotel in New York when I rang him. It was electrifying to hear him describe what he said he cooked for himself. For a long time, whenever I cooked an Italian dish, I played his 'O sole mio' and other Neapolitan songs.

Serves 2

2–4 garlic cloves, finely chopped

2 tbsp extra virgin olive oil

500g ripe plum tomatoes, peeled and chopped

½ tsp sugar, or to taste

2 tbsp torn fresh basil leaves

200g spaghetti

salt and black pepper

grated Parmesan, Pecorino sardo or Grana Padano, to serve

Fry the garlic in the oil until it just begins to colour. Add the tomatoes, sugar and some salt and pepper, then simmer for 8 minutes. Take off the heat and add the basil.

Cook the spaghetti in boiling salted water according to the packet instructions until al dente, then drain and toss with the sauce.

Serve with grated cheese.

FISH AND SEAFOOD

Until the early twentieth century, fish was considered food for the poor in Mediterranean countries. The wealthy and aristocratic were only interested in meat. Because of the high mountains and lack of transport in the hinterland, before roads were built, and before refrigeration, the only fish available in the interior was from rivers – trout, salmon, and eels – or salted cod. Fishermen could barely sell their fish; they fished for their own consumption. Many of the glorious fish and seafood dishes that developed with tourism are said to be inspired by what they cooked for themselves on boats or brought home for their wives to prepare. Fish soups especially, born from the leftovers of their catch, are seen as having gone from 'poor' to 'posh'. You only have to see the eager faces of people queuing at fish stalls in markets, who watch the fishmonger clean, fillet and prepare their wares with art and tenderness, to understand just how important and appreciated fish and seafood have become.

Mediterranean fishermen are often of mixed ethnic ancestry – Genoese, Neapolitan, Sicilian, Spanish, Greek, Tunisian – because they moved around. In Sicily, Arab words have been used in tuna fishing since early medieval times, and the port city of Trapani, famous for its fish couscous, has a Tunisian quarter, while a neighbouring fishing village has one called *la casbah*, which is home to a Tunisian community. In Sardinia, fishermen still speak thirteenth-century Catalan. In Gibraltar, many people have Genoese names because of the Genoese fishermen who settled there. I once planned a menu for the Gibraltar Literary Festival around the influences on Gibraltarian gastronomy. We had a dinner in advance in London to try the dishes and I spoke a few words about the origin of each dish. When I explained the Genoese legacy, the Gibraltarian High Commissioner, who was there, told us that his grandfather had been a fisherman from Genoa. This is also the reason why you can find similar fish dishes with similar-sounding names throughout the region.

The cities dotted all along the Mediterranean coastline like a necklace, the bustling seaports and fishing villages with their marinas and fish auctions, squares and markets and cafés, and mixtures of people and cultures, are a vibrant living proof of the unity and diversity of the Mediterranean universe that is so attractive to me. The dishes in this chapter are those that stayed with me, that I want to keep making for my friends and family.

EASY AÏOLI

The aïoli of Provence and its variations are served with many fish and shellfish dishes. I once made this garlicky mayonnaise with a pestle and mortar – it was laborious, but satisfying – and for years I made it with a simple whisk, not always successfully. When I saw someone make it with a hand blender in a tall thin jug, I couldn't believe it. This extremely easy way of making mayonnaise in a few minutes works perfectly. Hurray!

Makes 300ml

1 large egg
1 tbsp lemon juice
2–4 garlic cloves, to taste, crushed
pinch of salt
200ml sunflower oil
50ml extra virgin olive oil

Make sure everything is at room temperature: this is important. Remove the egg from the fridge 1 hour before you start.

Put the egg, lemon juice, garlic and salt in the blender goblet and pour in both oils. They will remain on top.

Put the blender right down to the bottom of the goblet and turn it on. Keep it down until the mixture becomes a pale thick cream that rises in the oil. Gently move the blender, still running, up and down until all the oil has been incorporated into a thick mayo.

Transfer to a bowl and keep, covered, in the fridge. It keeps well for a couple of weeks.

Variations

~ For *rouille*, add 1–2 teaspoons paprika or sweet *pimentón* and a good pinch of cayenne, or 1 tablespoon harissa.

~ For saffron aïoli, heat a good pinch of saffron threads in 1 tablespoon water and stir into the aïoli.

~ For green aïoli, add chopped herbs such as dill, chives, basil, mint and parsley.

~ For tomato aïoli, beat in 2 tablespoons tomato purée.

Making aïoli with good-quality mayonnaise

If you do not want to use raw egg, use 300ml good-quality bought 'real' mayonnaise and beat in 3 tablespoons extra virgin olive oil, the juice of ½ lemon and 2–4 crushed garlic cloves. You can also make the variations above in the same way.

LE GRAND AÏOLI

The French flag bunting around the square, the band playing *bal-musette* tango and polka, the long trestle table covered with paper, everyone helping themselves to salt cod, boiled vegetables, hard-boiled eggs and masses of shining aïoli. Can my aïoli dinner ever taste as good as the one that day at the *fête du village* in Lacoste in the Vaucluse? It does bring joy. The aïoli is the star. The usual vegetables are potatoes, carrots and green beans, but you can add others such as cauliflower, fennel, artichoke hearts, broccoli and courgettes. And fresh cod will do instead of salt cod.

Serves 6

2 x recipe quantities of aïoli (page 174)
6 waxy potatoes, scrubbed
6 carrots, peeled
600g green beans, topped and tailed and strung if necessary
1 cauliflower, divided into 6
6 hard-boiled eggs, cut in half lengthways
6 skinless cod loin fillets, about 750g
salt and black pepper
a bottle of extra virgin olive oil, to serve
fleur de sel (flaky sea salt), to serve

Prepare the aïoli and put it into two bowls. You can do this in advance and keep it covered in the fridge.

If you have a large enough pan you can cook all the vegetables together. Put in the potatoes and carrots, cover with plenty of water, add salt and bring to the boil. Simmer for 15 minutes, then add the green beans and cauliflower and simmer for about 6–8 minutes or until all the vegetables are tender. Drain and divide between two large platters, with the eggs.

Bring another pan of salted water to a gentle simmer and poach the fish for 2–5 minutes, until the flesh begins to flake. Drain and divide between the platters with the vegetables.

Serve hot or warm. Pass around the aïoli and olive oil for people to help themselves.

Have tiny bowls of flaky sea salt and a pepper pot on the table.

SEAFOOD JELLY

I was judging the best restaurant in Australia and worrying about the impossibility of deciding. Then, I had a dish called 'Rockpool' at Stephanie Alexander's in Melbourne. What you do with the memory of a dish often turns out to be entirely different from the one that inspired you. The flavours of my seafood jelly are those of Marseille and bouillabaisse. It is different every time I make it. Use seafood that you like, and can afford. It is not a firm jellied terrine that you unmould – it is soft. Make it in a wide serving dish and let it set in the fridge for at least 4 hours or overnight. It is one of my grand, very beautiful dishes.

Serve it with a homemade saffron aïoli or *rouille* (page 175), or with a good-quality bought mayonnaise. If you can't buy good fresh fish stock, use a fish stockpot.

Serves 6–8

1 litre fish stock

125ml dry white wine

250g skinless white fish fillets, such as cod or monkfish

260g raw peeled king prawns

200g small wild Atlantic scallops

3 thyme sprigs, leaves only

2 bay leaves

1 tsp fennel seeds

strips of peel from ½ orange

pinch of saffron threads or good-quality saffron powder

1 tbsp lemon juice

1 tsp sugar

3 tbsp pastis, arak, raki or ouzo (optional)

6 gelatine leaves

bunch (25g) of flat-leaf parsley, leaves chopped

small bunch (15g) of dill, chopped

salt and black pepper

In a large pan, bring the fish stock and white wine to a gentle simmer. Very briefly poach the seafood, one type at a time, until barely cooked – the fish until it just begins to flake when you cut into it, the prawns until they turn pink, the scallops for seconds only (they are best when they are slightly underdone). Lift them out with a slotted spoon and put them aside.

Add the thyme, bay, fennel seeds, orange peel, saffron, lemon juice, sugar and pastis, if using, to the fish stock. Cover and simmer over low heat for 15–20 minutes, tasting to check the seasoning. Strain the liquid through a fine sieve into a large measuring jug; it should come up to about 800ml. If not, add a little water and check the seasoning again. Return to the pan and heat through, then turn off the heat and let it cool for 10 minutes.

Soak the gelatine leaves in a bowl of cold water for 4–5 minutes – they will swell slightly and become soft. Squeeze out the excess water and drop them into the fish stock. Stir vigorously until they have dissolved.

Wet a wide serving dish or bowl and pour in the stock. Put in the seafood, parsley and dill and gently mix. Leave to cool, then cover and leave in the fridge for at least 4 hours or overnight, until set.

Serve chilled or at room temperature.

FISH TARTARE WITH TOMATO VINAIGRETTE

Raw salmon dressed with a Catalan *vinagreta de tomàquet* and accompanied by a little bowl of mayonnaise is heaven. In Arab culinary lore, I have often encountered dishes 'you make when you love somebody'. This is one such dish for me.

You must use ultra fresh fish – not from a supermarket. I get my salmon from my local Japanese mini market, where they sell it sliced for sashimi or will slice it for you.

Serves 4

300g very fresh raw salmon, sliced for sashimi
4 tbsp mild fruity extra virgin olive oil
grated zest of 1 lemon and juice of ½ lemon
½ tsp runny honey
1 large beef tomato, about 150g
2 handfuls of small salad leaves, to serve
2 tbsp snipped fresh chives
2 tbsp chopped fresh dill
salt and black pepper, to taste

Buy the fish on the day you want to serve it and keep it covered in the fridge until you are ready to serve.

Make the tomato dressing as the Catalans do: put the olive oil in a bowl, add the lemon zest and juice, the honey and some salt and pepper and beat well with a fork. Cut the tomato in half crossways and grate through the large holes of a grater into the bowl, pressing hard and leaving the skin behind. Stir with the fork to mix the tomato with the dressing.

Arrange the salmon slices on individual plates with some salad leaves on the side. Pour over the dressing and sprinkle with the chives and dill.

Lemon and chilli garlic mayonnaise

Beat 100ml good-quality bought mayonnaise with 1 tablespoon lemon juice, 1 crushed garlic clove and a pinch of chilli or cayenne pepper to taste. Alternatively, use 100ml homemade aïoli (see page 175).

CRAB SALAD

My mother's cool and glamorous cousin Edith, who lived in Swiss Cottage, asked: 'Do you want a crab?' I had gone to see her for family recipes, but crab was not one of them. She took me to the fishmonger, where she bought a large live crab. I have eaten and cooked many crabs since – crabcakes, gratins, salads – but it's the simplicity of Edith's crab salad that is so appealing.

You can buy white crab meat in supermarkets; it is expensive but worth it. It has such a delicate flavour that you need a mild extra virgin olive oil.

Serves 2

80g white crab meat
a handful of rocket leaves
1 tomato, finely diced
1 spring onion (white part), sliced
½–1 tbsp lemon juice
2 tbsp mild extra virgin olive oil
1 tbsp freshly chopped flat-leaf parsley
salt and black pepper, to taste

Divide the crab meat between two plates and arrange the rocket, diced tomato and spring onion around it.

Whisk together the lemon juice, olive oil and some salt and pepper and dress the salad. Serve sprinkled with the parsley.

HARICOT BEANS WITH CLAMS

One night on the seafront in Barcelona, I was looking for a restaurant that served *zarzuela*. I had eaten the extraordinary seafood stew many years before and it had left such an impression that I was desperately keen to have it again. My friend Pepa Aymami, who lives in Barcelona, only wanted clams. My *zarzuela* was disappointing but Pepa's clams were delicious.

The Spanish *alubias con almejas* is my favourite clam recipe. Use good-quality white haricot beans from a jar or tin. The wine gives them a delicate flavour and the clams add the taste of the sea.

Serves 2

650g clams
3 tbsp olive oil
1 large onion, chopped
½ small fresh chilli, chopped (optional)
3–4 garlic cloves, finely chopped
350g jar small white haricot beans (or 1 x 400g tin), drained and rinsed
125ml fruity white wine or cava
2 tbsp chopped flat-leaf parsley
salt

Throw away any clams that are chipped or broken and any open ones that do not close when you tap them on the sink or dip them in ice-cold water. Scrub them with a brush if they are dirty. Leave them in fresh cold water for 20 minutes – as they breathe they will push out any sand that remains inside. Lift them out and rinse them in a colander under running water.

Heat the oil in a wide casserole or pan with a tight-fitting lid. Add the onion and the chilli, if using, and stir over low heat until very soft and beginning to colour. Add the garlic and stir for a minute or so.

Add the beans, the wine and a little salt, mix gently and cook for 2–3 minutes. Put the clams on top, put the lid on, and cook over medium–high heat for 2–3 minutes until the clams open. Throw away any that do not open. Serve sprinkled with parsley.

OCTOPUS IN RED WINE AND POTATO SALAD

It was late summer on the Greek island of Skopelos. Men were bashing octopus on rocks to tenderise them and then hanging them up on lines. As I was walking past a family eating on their terrace, they invited me in to share their octopus salad and a bottle of wine. It was heaven. In my version, cooked in red wine, the octopus acquires a delicate flavour and rich colour.

In Britain, octopuses are usually sold cleaned and frozen (freezing tenderises them). A 1kg octopus might look huge when you buy it, but it will shrink enormously when you cook it. Defrost it completely before cooking – you can let it thaw overnight in the fridge.

Serves 6

1 octopus (about 1–1.25kg), defrosted if frozen

300ml red wine

2 tbsp wine vinegar

2 tsp sugar

500g waxy new potatoes

6 tbsp extra virgin olive oil

2 tbsp lemon juice

good pinch of chilli pepper (optional)

1 tbsp chopped flat-leaf parsley

salt and black pepper

Wash the octopus under cold running water inside and out. Cut away the head and cut out the central beak, if it has not already been removed, and throw them away. Half-fill a very large pan with water and bring to the boil. Throw in the octopus and blanch for 3 minutes until it firms and the tentacles curl up gracefully, then drain.

Put it back in the empty pan and add the wine, vinegar, sugar and some salt and pepper. Add just enough water to cover and simmer gently for about 45–60 minutes, or until it feels very tender when you pierce the top of a tentacle with a pointed knife. Let it cool in the cooking broth, then drain. Lift it out of the pan and cut the tentacles into 3cm pieces, leaving the thin ends longer.

While the octopus is cooking, peel the potatoes and cook them in boiling salted water until tender. Drain and cut them into slices about 1.5cm thick.

For the dressing, beat the oil with the lemon juice, some salt and pepper, and the chilli pepper if using. Dress the potatoes and the octopus pieces separately, using half of the dressing for each. Mix them together and serve at room temperature, sprinkled with parsley.

CREAMED SALT COD, POTATOES AND GARLIC

Even when they lived by the sea, many people I spoke to said their favourite fish was salt cod: *morue* in France, *baccalà* in Italy, and *bacalao* in Spain and Portugal.

Cod is not a fish of Mediterranean waters and you may wonder why a dried fish is so popular in coastal areas. Since the tenth century, fishermen have been going out to the North Atlantic to get cod. They fillet it on their boats, stack the fillets between layers of salt to extract the moisture, and dry them. The Christian countries became addicted to the strong, distinctive taste when it was used as a replacement for meat during Lent and other fasting days, at a time when fresh fish was unobtainable in the interior due to lack of transport and refrigeration. The old traditional penitential dishes are now much-loved delicacies.

You can find salt cod in Iberian and Italian stores, usually in 300g packs. It needs to be soaked in cold water for around 24 hours before you can use it.

My very favourite salt cod dish is *brandade*. I used to buy it from the market in the Rue de Seine in Paris and eat it, still hot, sitting on a bench in a little garden where people went to scatter bread for birds.

Serve it as an appetiser spread on small pieces of thin toast brushed with extra virgin olive oil, or as a first course accompanied by a green salad.

Serves 6

300g salt cod
2 large floury potatoes (about 300g), peeled and quartered
125ml double cream or whole milk, warmed
125ml extra virgin olive oil
1–3 garlic cloves, crushed
juice of ½ lemon (optional)
2–3 tbsp snipped fresh chives, to garnish (optional)
salt and black pepper

Soak the salt cod in plenty of cold water for 24 hours, changing the water at least four times.

Boil the potatoes in salted water until soft, then drain.

Place the desalted and drained salt cod in a pan of cold water and bring to simmering point, then remove the pan from the heat and let it stand for 15 minutes. Drain, then carefully remove any skin and bones (there are usually quite a few), and flake into small pieces with your fingers.

Put the fish in a food processor and blend to a paste. Then pour in the cream or milk and oil, a little at a time, alternating them, and pulse to a creamy paste.

Add garlic and pepper to taste, then add the boiled potatoes and blend briefly to a creamy purée that retains a little texture. If you have over-soaked the fish and desalted it too much you may need to add a little salt. You may also like to add a little lemon juice.

If serving cold, spoon into a bowl and sprinkle with chives. If you want to serve it hot, preheat the oven to 180°C/160°C fan/gas 4. Spoon the *brandade* into a baking dish and bake for 10 minutes.

CCALA
GIOVA
ARGE -
2,80 A

BABY SQUID IN THEIR INK WITH VERMICELLI AND AÏOLI

I discovered short, thin pasta cooked in a paella pan with seafood on the Valencian coast of Spain, where my friend Alicia Ríos had a house overlooking the sea. My favourite version is the mesmerising *chipirones en su tinta con fideus* – short, thin pasta in a shiny black sauce with tiny squid and a fantastic taste of the sea. It is easy to make. I use dried vermicelli nests, but you can also use short thin wheat noodles.

Many fishmongers and some supermarkets sell frozen packs of baby squid not more than 6–7cm long, cleaned and packed with the tentacles inside the bodies. Some also sell sachets of concentrated cuttlefish or squid ink. I serve this with aïoli (page 175).

Serves 4

800g pack frozen prepared baby squid, defrosted

1 large onion, chopped

4–5 tbsp olive oil

2 garlic cloves, crushed

1 very large or 2 medium tomatoes (about 200g), peeled and chopped

150ml dry white wine

450ml fish stock (use 1 fish stockpot)

½ tsp sugar

2–3 squid ink sachets

200g dried vermicelli nests or short fine wheat noodles

2 tbsp chopped flat-leaf parsley (optional)

salt and black pepper

Drain the defrosted squid, take the tentacles out of the bodies, and slice the bodies into rings about 1cm wide.

In a large pan over low heat, fry the onion in 2 tablespoons of the oil, covered with a lid but stirring often, for 10–15 minutes until soft and golden. Add the garlic and cook, stirring, until the aroma rises and it just begins to colour. Add the tomato and cook for 5–8 minutes, stirring often, then add the wine and the fish stock, the sugar and some salt (taking into consideration the saltiness of the fish stock) and pepper. Simmer over low heat for 10 minutes, then add the squid ink (3 sachets will make the sauce blacker).

In a large frying pan, heat the remaining oil over medium heat and fry the squid rings and the tentacles for about 10 minutes, stirring and turning the pieces over.

Crush the vermicelli into small pieces in your hand and throw them into the ink sauce. Cook for 3–6 minutes, with the lid on, stirring often until done. Add the squid rings and tentacles, scatter with the parsley, if using, and serve hot, with aïoli.

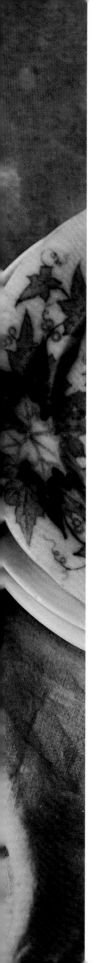

SPAGHETTI WITH PRAWNS PROVENÇAL

There are many versions of pasta with seafood around the Mediterranean sea. When, for a Sunday paper, I asked Italian celebrities what their favourite pasta dish was, most said *'ai frutti di mare'* and that it was their own recipe. I tried them and loved them all. But for *my* favourite, I cook the pasta a Catalan way in boiling fish stock (it adds a surprise layer of flavour) and serve with a sauce from the Côte d'Azur. My grandson Cesar, a pasta man, adds a lot of chilli. I sometimes add other seafood, such as squid or shellfish.

Serves 4

500g ripe tomatoes

1 onion, chopped

2 tbsp olive oil

3 garlic cloves, chopped

200ml dry white wine

3 thyme sprigs, leaves only

1–2 tsp sugar

good pinch of chilli pepper

500g raw peeled king prawns

2 fish stockpots

400g spaghetti

2 tbsp extra virgin olive oil

3 tbsp chopped flat-leaf parsley

salt

Quarter the tomatoes, and remove the little white hard bits at the stem end. Blend them to a creamy consistency in a food processor.

In a wide pan, over low heat, fry the onion in the olive oil, stirring often, until it is very soft. Add the garlic, and when it begins to colour, add the blended tomatoes and the wine, thyme, sugar, chilli and some salt. Simmer, uncovered, for about 20 minutes, until the sauce is reduced and aromatic. Add the prawns and cook for 1 minute more until they turn pink.

Bring a large pan of water to the boil, add the fish stockpots and some salt (not too much salt as the stockpots are already salty) and stir to dissolve them. Put in the spaghetti and cook until al dente, then drain.

Serve the pasta with the sauce poured over, a drizzle of extra virgin olive oil, and a sprinkling of parsley.

PAN-GRILLED FISH WITH GARLIC, VINEGAR AND CHILLI

This simple fish dish is fabulous. In Spain, I would eat a whole fish, cooked open like a book a *la espalda* in the pan, with this dressing, but fillets will do very well. Use hake, bream or sea bass, with the skin on. Serve with herby mashed potatoes with olive oil (page 123) or, for a quick store-cupboard side, the white cannellini beans opposite. You can make it for more people by roasting the fillets in the oven (see the note).

Serves 2

2 hake, bream or sea bass fillets, skin on

4 tbsp extra virgin olive oil

5 large garlic cloves, sliced

good pinch of chilli pepper

2–3 tsp sherry vinegar or white wine vinegar

1 tbsp chopped flat-leaf parsley

salt

Season the fish with salt. Heat 1 tablespoon of the oil in a heavy non-stick frying pan. Put the fillets in, skin-side down, and press them down with a spatula to flatten them as the skin curls. Cook over low–medium heat until the skin is crisp and lightly browned. They will gradually cook through almost to the top. The timing depends on the type and thickness of the fish, and will take 2–5 minutes, but do not overcook: they are done when the flesh flakes when you cut into the thickest part with a pointed knife. Turn and cook the flesh side for a few seconds more.

For the dressing, in a small pan, gently heat the remaining 3 tablespoons of oil with the garlic and chilli until the garlic is only just lightly golden and crunchy (do not let it get brown). Take off the heat and add the vinegar, to taste.

Serve the fish very hot, with the dressing poured over, sprinkled with parsley.

White cannellini beans

Fry a chopped onion in 1 tablespoon of oil over low heat, stirring, for 5 minutes, until soft and beginning to colour. Drain a 400g tin cannellini beans, rinse, then add to the onion. Season with salt and pepper, add a few fresh thyme leaves and 100ml water and cook, covered, for 5 minutes. Serve with a drizzle of 1–2 tablespoons extra virgin olive oil.

Note

If you want to serve more than two people, you can make this as a tray bake. Preheat the oven to 200°C/180°C fan/gas 6. Lay the fish fillets skin-side down in an oiled baking tray, brush them with oil, season with salt and cook for 12–15 minutes. Make the dressing as opposite, multiplying the rest of the ingredients.

RED MULLET WITH PROVENÇAL MASHED POTATOES

Red mullet is often paired with black olives. They bring out its rosy tint and unique delicate flavour. There are olives and sun-dried tomatoes in the mashed potatoes and sometimes I make an olive paste to dab on the fish (see variation). The red mullet I find at the fishmonger is usually in large fillets, not the small whole fish.

Serves 4

750g floury potatoes, peeled

6 tbsp extra virgin olive oil, or a half-and-half mix of olive and sunflower oil

16 black olives, coarsely chopped

16 semi-dried tomatoes in oil, coarsely chopped

1 fresh chilli, finely chopped (optional)

good handful of chopped herbs, such as parsley, chives and dill

2 tbsp olive oil, for frying

4 large red mullet fillets, skin on

salt and black pepper

Boil the potatoes in salted water until soft. Drain, keeping about 150ml of the cooking water. Mash them and beat in the oil. Add salt and pepper to taste and just enough of the cooking water to give a soft, slightly moist mash. Then stir in the olives, tomatoes, the chilli if using, and the herbs and mix well.

Heat the oil in a non-stick frying pan. Put the fillets in, skin-side down, and cook over medium heat for about 3 minutes, then turn them over and cook for 30 seconds or until cooked through.

Serve the fish with the mashed potatoes and, if you like, some olivade to dab on the fish.

Olivade

For an olive paste to serve with the fish, blend 100g pitted black olives with 1 crushed garlic clove, 100ml extra virgin olive oil and 1 tablespoon sherry vinegar.

FISH À LA PROVENÇALE IN TOMATO SAUCE

The enticing mingled aromas of ginger, saffron, orange and lemon peel, honey and chilli are of Provence. They make one of the most luscious sauces for fish I know. You can use any white fish such as monkfish, hake or cod, and also salmon steaks or thick fillets. Use this sauce also with grilled, tray-baked or roasted fish.

Serves 4

1kg ripe tomatoes or 2 x 400g tins plum tomatoes

5 tbsp olive oil

4 garlic cloves, chopped

good pinch of saffron threads

1–1¼ tsp ground ginger

grated zest of ½ orange

grated zest of ½ lemon

1½ tbsp runny honey

good pinch of chilli pepper, to taste

4 thick skinless fish fillets or steaks

plain flour, to coat the fish

4 tbsp chopped flat-leaf parsley

12 good-quality black olives (optional)

1 tbsp drained capers (optional)

salt and black pepper

Wash the tomatoes, quarter them, and remove the little white hard bits at the stem end. Blend them to a creamy consistency in a food processor.

In a wide pan, heat 2 tablespoons of the oil over low heat, add the garlic and stir for less than a minute, until the aroma rises and the garlic just begins to colour. Add the blended tomatoes, saffron, ginger, grated zests and some salt. Stir well and simmer for about 10 minutes until the tomatoes are reduced. Add the honey, and chilli pepper to taste, and cook, stirring, for a few moments more.

Season the fish with salt and pepper. Put a generous amount of flour on a plate and turn the fish fillets in this to coat them all over, then shake vigorously to remove excess flour.

Heat the remaining oil in a non-stick frying pan over medium heat. Put in the fish and cook for 3–4 minutes (or up to 10 minutes), depending on the fish and the thickness of the fillets, turning them over once, until lightly browned and just cooked through. If you make it with salmon, which I often use, it should be slightly underdone.

Serve the fish on the sauce, sprinkled with parsley and garnished, if you like, with chopped olives and capers.

Variation

For an intriguing anise flavour, add 3 tablespoons pastis, raki or ouzo to the sauce at the same time as the flavourings.

SALMON COOKED IN FOIL WITH SALSA VERDE

When we are at my daughter Anna's house, she often cooks a whole salmon. She serves it hot with boiled new potatoes and this refreshing Italian salsa verde. Hot or cold, it is the perfect lunch on a summer's day. Cooking the fish in foil keeps the flesh moist and juicy. It is beautiful – pale pink against the bright green salsa.

Ask the fishmonger to fillet and skin the fish and keep the head to use for presentation.

Serves 8–10

2 tbsp olive oil

1 whole salmon, about 2.5kg, filleted and skinned

150ml dry white wine

salt and black pepper

Salsa verde

large bunch (75g) of flat-leaf parsley, stems removed

75g pine nuts

5 small gherkins

8 pitted green olives

3 garlic cloves, crushed

3 tbsp wine vinegar or the juice of ½ lemon

200–250ml very mild extra virgin olive oil

Preheat the oven to 200°C/180°C fan/gas 6.

Lay a large sheet of heavy-duty double-width foil in a roasting tin (or double up two thinner sheets), brush with the oil and place the two salmon fillets together, one on top of the other. Season with salt and pepper. Bring the edges of the foil up over the fish to surround it and pour in the wine. Fold the foil edges together to make a sealed baggy parcel (it should not be tight). Wrap the head in another piece of greased foil and put it in the roasting tin.

Place the roasting tin in the oven and cook for about 30–40 minutes. Salmon is best a little underdone, so check after 30 minutes – open the foil parcel and cut into the thickest part of the fish with the point of a knife. The flesh should flake but should still be translucent in the centre. If serving cold, leave the fish to cool in the foil parcel.

For the salsa verde, put all the ingredients except the oil in a food processor, with some salt and pepper, and blend, gradually adding the oil to make a light paste.

Serve the salmon hot or cold; put the head in place at the top of the fish.

FRIED FISH WITH CUMIN AND TAHINI SAUCE

I was sitting in a restaurant in Tripoli in Lebanon, overlooking the sea, eating fried fish. The crisp sea bream with a delicate lemony tahini sauce, the smell of the sea, the gentle breeze and brilliant light took me back to Xenophon, the Greek fish restaurant in Alexandria where we always stopped on our arrival from Cairo when I was a child. The joy of it! I wanted to cry.

Serve this with herby mashed potatoes with olive oil (page 123).

Serves 4

4 firm white fish fillets, such as bream or sea bass, skinless

3 tbsp plain flour, to coat the fish

1–1½ tsp ground cumin

2 tbsp olive oil, for frying

1 tbsp chopped flat-leaf parsley

1 lemon, quartered, to serve

salt

Tahini sauce

3 tbsp tahini

juice of ½–1 lemon

1 small garlic clove, crushed (optional)

For the tahini sauce, stir the tahini in the jar before putting 3 tablespoonfuls in a small serving bowl. Gradually add the lemon juice and 2–3 tablespoons water, beating vigorously with a fork and adding just enough water to get the consistency of a runny cream. The paste will stiffen at first and then become light and smooth. Add a little salt to taste, and the garlic, if using.

Season the fish with salt. Put the flour, cumin and a pinch of salt on a plate and mix well. Turn the fish fillets in this to coat them all over, then shake vigorously to remove excess flour.

Heat a small amount of oil in a non-stick frying pan. Put the fillets in and cook over medium heat, turning them over once, for 3–10 minutes depending on their thickness, until crisp, lightly browned and just cooked through (the flesh should be opaque when you gently cut in with a pointed knife).

Serve the fish with a sprinkling of parsley and the lemon quarters. Pass the tahini sauce around for people to help themselves.

BRODETTO

A fish soup is immensely satisfying. Everyone is happy with this very simple Italian *brodetto*. You find versions of it all around the coasts of Italy. You need a firm-fleshed fish, ideally monkfish, but others will do too. When my grandson Cesar made it, his fishmonger suggested cod cheeks were good for a soup, and they were.

Serves 4

400ml dry white wine

600ml fish stock, or water plus 1 fish stockpot

350g new potatoes, peeled and sliced

250g tomatoes, peeled and cut in big pieces

4 garlic cloves, chopped

2 fresh red chillies (optional)

2 tsp sugar, or to taste

500g skinless fish fillets, such as monkfish

salt

bread, to serve

chilli pepper, to serve

Put the wine and stock or water in a large pan. Add the stockpot, if using, then add the potatoes, tomatoes, garlic and chillies, if using.

Bring to the boil and simmer for 30 minutes, adding sugar and salt to taste. Remove the chillies, if using, when you feel the soup is spicy enough.

Just before serving, add the fish fillets and cook for 5–10 minutes until they just begin to flake when you cut into them with a pointed knife.

Serve the soup with bread and pass the chilli pepper around for people to serve themselves if they want to.

BULLINADA

The Catalan *bullinada* is like the *bourride* of the French Riviera and the *gazpachuelo* of Malaga – a fish soup with garlic mayonnaise stirred in. It has a mysterious delicate flavour and beautiful warm colour. It is sometimes made with tiny baby squid alone, or a mix of prawns and shellfish. I make it with white fish alone for friends who cannot eat shellfish. Use hake, monkfish or cod cheeks. You can make much of it in advance and finish the soup a few minutes before you are ready to eat.

Serves 6

1 large onion, chopped

2 tbsp olive oil

8 garlic cloves: 6 finely chopped and 2 crushed

good pinch of saffron threads

2 litres fish stock (use 3 fish stockpots)

100ml dry white wine

800g new potatoes, peeled and cut into 1.5cm slices

1 tsp fennel seeds

strips of peel from ½ orange

800g skinless fish fillets, such as hake or monkfish

200ml good-quality bought mayonnaise

juice of ½ lemon

good pinch of chilli pepper, plus extra to serve

4 tbsp chopped flat-leaf parsley

salt and black pepper

In a wide pan, fry the onion in the oil over low heat, stirring occasionally, for 5 minutes until it begins to soften. Add the chopped garlic and stir for 2 minutes until it just begins to colour.

Stir in the saffron and pour in the fish stock and the wine, then put in the potatoes, fennel seeds and orange peel and season with salt and pepper. Simmer, covered, for 20–25 minutes until the potatoes are tender.

Ten minutes before you are ready to serve, remove the orange peel and put in the fish. Cook, covered, over low heat for 4–10 minutes, depending on the fish and the thickness of the fillets, until the fish becomes opaque and the flesh begins to flake when you cut into it with a pointed knife. Break the fillets into pieces.

In a jug, beat the mayonnaise with the lemon juice, the crushed garlic and a pinch of chilli.

Just before serving, add a ladleful or two of the hot stock into the mayonnaise mixture and beat it in, then gently stir into the simmering soup. Heat through but do not let it boil or the mayonnaise will curdle. Serve sprinkled with parsley and pass round some chilli for anyone who would like to add more.

BOUILLABAISSE

Bouillabaisse belongs to the most colourful, bustling, cosmopolitan, multicultural port city of the Mediterranean – Marseille. Starting as a fisherman's way of using fish that have not sold, it became a trendy delicacy and something of an event. This easy, accessible bouillabaisse does not have the bony *rascasse* and other traditional fish, crustaceans and shellfish you may find in Marseille, but it does have the magnificent flavours. Using good-quality bought fish stock or a stockpot means you can concentrate on the aromatics. You can make most of it in advance but you have to be ready to deal with two or three pans at the same time 15 minutes before serving. The optional clams and mussels are cooked separately; keep them in the fridge until you are ready to use them. Serve the soup with the homemade aïoli or *rouille* (page 175) or the easy saffron aïoli opposite spread on lightly toasted bread.

Serves 4–6

1 litre good-quality fish stock or use 1 stockpot

½ onion, chopped

½ fennel bulb with feathery leaves, chopped

1 large tomato

3 thyme sprigs, leaves only

2 bay leaves

1 tsp fennel seeds

grated zest of ½ orange

good pinch of saffron threads

125ml dry white wine

1 tsp sugar, to taste

4 tbsp pastis or another anise-flavoured spirit such as arak, raki or ouzo

500g waxy new potatoes

500g–1kg clams or mussels (optional)

500g white fish fillets, such as monkfish or bream

140g raw peeled king prawns

bunch of flat-leaf parsley, leaves chopped

salt and black pepper

Heat the fish stock in a large pan and put in the onion, fennel, tomato, thyme, bay leaves, fennel seeds, orange zest, saffron and wine and simmer for 30–45 minutes. Add a teaspoon of sugar if you like and the pastis, arak, raki or ouzo at the end.

Cook the potatoes in boiling salted water until tender, then drain. When cool enough to handle, peel them – or not, as you like – and cut them into slices. Return them to the pan.

If using clams or mussels, wash them in plenty of cold water (pull off the 'beards' from the mussels) and throw away any that are broken and any open ones that do not close when you tap them on the sink or dip them in ice-cold water. Scrub them with a brush if they are dirty. Leave them for 20 minutes in fresh cold water – as they breathe they will push out any sand that remains inside. Lift them out and rinse them in cold water.

About 15 minutes before you are ready to serve, reheat the stock. Put in the fish and seafood and simmer until cooked through. Monkfish takes 10–15 minutes so put it in first; the prawns take 2 minutes so put them in last. Cut the fish into chunks.

At the same time, pour a few tablespoons of the fish stock over the potatoes and heat through with the lid on.

Put the clams or mussels in a pan with less than a finger of water, put the pan over high heat and put the lid on. As soon as they open (within a minute or two), remove them from the heat – they are cooked. Throw away any that haven't opened.

Serve the bouillabaisse in soup bowls – potatoes at the bottom and shellfish on top, sprinkled with parsley.

Lemony saffron aïoli

Beat 125ml good-quality 'real' mayonnaise with the juice of ½ lemon and 1–2 crushed garlic cloves. Heat a good pinch of saffron threads in 1 tablespoon of water and stir into the aïoli.

SICILIAN FISH *CUSCUSU IMPERIALE* OF TRAPANI

I was on the jury of a couscous competition in San Vito lo Capo, near Trapani in Sicily. There was always an annual local *festa del couscous*, then it went international and every country that has a couscous tradition was invited to participate. The streets were in carnival mood with lights, musicians, cooking demonstrations and tastings. The competition was carried out with pomp and ceremony. Each delegation marched with their couscous on a big tray and their flag, accompanied by their national anthem. The Italians won. Their fish *cuscusu* was sublime. It is the local dish in the little fishing-village-turned-holiday-resort of Trapani, where all kinds of seafood are used. Songs and poems are written about it and it features in legends and proverbs.

When I celebrated my eightieth birthday with the family in Sicily I had a simpler version in a restaurant, which I've tried to reproduce. It is worth making for a lot of people and easy to double the quantities. As well as the grain and a stock in which you poach the seafood, there's the fresh tomato and almond pesto *trapanese*, which can be delicate and aromatic, but if you like it hot you can use plenty of chilli; it can be made in advance and kept, covered, in the fridge.

Serves 4

800ml good-quality fish stock or use 1 stockpot

150ml dry white wine

good pinch of saffron threads

250g couscous

1 tbsp extra virgin olive oil

grated zest of ½ orange

300g skinless fish fillets, such as monkfish or hake

200g raw peeled king prawns

salt, to taste

Trapani pesto

400g ripe plum tomatoes

1–4 garlic cloves, crushed, to taste

1 tsp sugar

¾ tsp ground ginger

4 tbsp extra virgin olive oil

salt

very good pinch of chilli pepper or dried chilli flakes, to taste

50g flaked almonds

bunch (25g) of basil, leaves chopped

Heat the fish stock with the wine and saffron. Put the couscous in a wide baking dish in which you can serve it and pour in 300ml of the fish stock, stirring well so that it is absorbed evenly. Leave for about 15 minutes, stirring again once or twice, until the grain has absorbed the liquid and is tender. Stir in the oil and rub the grains between your hands above the dish to aerate the couscous and break up any lumps.

For the Trapani pesto, you do not need to peel the tomatoes. Cut them into quarters and remove the little white hard bits at the stem end. Put them in a food processor with the garlic, sugar, ginger, oil, a little salt and the chilli, and blend to a creamy consistency. Add the almonds and basil leaves and blend briefly until the almonds are very coarsely chopped.

Preheat the oven to 200°C/180°C fan/gas 6. Cover the dish of couscous with foil. Ten minutes before serving put the couscous in the oven to reheat. Bring the remaining fish stock to the boil, taste and adjust the seasoning and add the orange zest. Put in the fish and simmer for 5 minutes, then add the prawns and cook for 1–2 minutes more until they turn pink.

To serve, pour the pesto all over the hot couscous and arrange the fish and seafood on top. Pour some broth over each serving.

MEAT AND POULTRY

I could tell by the aromas wafting from behind the walls what spices were being used, and at what stage the cooking was. In the labyrinth of alleys in the *medina*, someone was roasting lamb, someone was frying fish, somewhere a tagine was beginning to sizzle and caramelise. I was in Fez to speak at a festival celebrating the regional cooking of Morocco and one of the helpers had invited me to her home. I arrived at a tiny door in a windowless mud-coloured wall. I thought it might lead into a hovel, but it opened into a paradise – a perfumed garden lined with cobalt and turquoise mosaics, with orange and lemon trees, a fig tree, vines and jasmine. It was the courtyard of an old *riad* that had seen better days but was all the more glorious and moving for that. We sat on low sofas in an alcove eating *kemias* (appetisers) while cone-shaped clay pots cooked gently on primus stoves in the courtyard. When it came, the *tagine* was heaven. The sharpness of the fruit married with spices and a touch of honey to give the meltingly tender lamb a mysterious, delicate flavour.

Meat is the prestige food of the Mediterranean and chicken is the popular everyday food. The area is sheep country and the usual meat is lamb and mutton. In Christian countries, the cooking of the mountain interior is dominated by the pig. There is not enough humidity nor the right terrain for cattle raising – traditionally, beef is used in small quantities in fillings or stuffings. There are goats; ducks and geese are part of the scenery around marshlands and rivers; pigeons and rabbits are raised; hare, wild boar and wild birds are hunted; the sea is the route of millions of migrating quails, whose arrival, tired, on the beaches is the gastronomic event of the season. I have many recipes for all of these, but I included here the most accessible meats and poultry because that is what we all want to cook.

Many of the recipes in this chapter are inspired by the eastern and southern Mediterranean. I love their celebratory dishes, their slow-roasted and long-braised lamb, their delicately spiced meats and those cooked with fruit. The area was on the early spice route from the East. It was the transit area, and the middlemen, the intermediaries, succumbed to the attractions of their merchandise. Each country has its favourites and its own special spice mixes. I always head for the spice street in the *souk* or bazaar. If you have ever walked through a spice street, you can never forget the intoxicating effect of the mingled scents and the extraordinary displays of red, brown and golden powders, the knotted roots, bits of bark and wood, shrivelled pods, seeds, berries, translucent resins, and curious-looking plants, bulbs, buds, petals and stigmas. I always used to bring home as much as I could from trips. Now that I buy spices in London, I imagine the spice shops in Marrakesh and Istanbul.

When you use spices and aromatics, my advice is to start with little and to add more if you wish, after you have tasted, and that includes chilli.

CHICKEN TRAY BAKE WITH OLIVES AND BOILED LEMON

The enticing aromas of mingled garlic, turmeric and ginger here are the same as those that waft over the food stalls every night in Place Djemaa el Fna, the great square in Marrakesh that during the day is taken over by Berber musicians, storytellers, comedians, fire eaters and snake charmers.

The sharp lemony flavours of one of the most famous Moroccan tagines work marvellously in this bake. It is very saucy and can be served with plain couscous (see overleaf) or with mashed potatoes (page 123). It is the kind of easy dish I make when I have many guests.

Serves 8

juice of 2 lemons

6 tbsp olive oil

1½ tsp ground turmeric

1½ tsp ground ginger

1½ tbsp honey

250ml dry white wine

1 whole head of garlic, cloves chopped

16 chicken thighs, bone in, skin on

120g capers in brine, drained

200g pitted green olives

1 large or 2 small unwaxed boiled lemons (see overleaf), cut into pieces, discarding the pips

bunch (25g) of coriander, leaves chopped

salt and black pepper

Preheat the oven to 180°C/160°C fan/gas 4.

In a large bowl, mix the lemon juice, olive oil, turmeric, ginger, honey, wine and some salt and pepper, beating well. Add the garlic and turn the chicken pieces in the mixture so that they are well coated.

Arrange the chicken thighs in a large roasting tin or baking dish in which they fit snugly, putting the capers, olives and boiled lemon pieces in between, and pour the liquid contents of the bowl all over. Bake for 1 hour or until the chicken is well browned and cooked through.

Serve sprinkled with chopped coriander.

Variation

Add frozen artichoke bottoms to the bake with the olives and capers. You can find them in Middle Eastern stores in packs of 9, weighing 400g.

Boiled lemons

Put whole unwaxed lemons in a pan with water to cover. Put a smaller lid on top to keep them down as they float, and boil for about 30 minutes or until they are very soft when you press them. If you don't use them right away, drain them and leave to cool. Pack them whole, pressing them into a jar, and cover with olive or sunflower oil. They will last a few weeks in the fridge. You can use them cut into pieces or blended to a paste.

Basic couscous

To serve 8, put 500g couscous into a large baking dish. Add ½–1 teaspoon of salt to 600ml warm water (half boiling, half cold) and gradually pour this all over the couscous, stirring so that it will be absorbed evenly. Leave to swell for 10 minutes, stirring a couple of times, then mix in 2 tablespoons of olive oil and rub the couscous between your hands above the dish to aerate the grains and break up any lumps. Cover with foil and place in the oven below the chicken for the last 10–15 minutes of the cooking time.

CHICKEN WITH GRAPES

When I asked people in Spain and in Italy what their favourite dishes were, several said chicken with grapes. I ate it in Tuscany with sweet wine and have made it many times that way, but in the end I prefer it without wine. Instead, the juices bursting out of the grapes come together with the chicken fat and juices to create a little sauce full of flavour.

This is lovely on a bed of polenta. Both can be made in advance and heated through before serving.

Serves 4

4 tbsp olive oil

2 rosemary sprigs, leaves only, chopped

8 chicken thighs, bone in, skin on

8 whole garlic cloves, peeled

500g seedless red grapes

salt and black pepper

Heat the oil in a large sauté pan wide enough to hold the chicken pieces in one layer. Put in the chopped rosemary and then the chicken, skin-side down. Season with salt and pepper and cook, covered, over medium heat until the skin is browned and has released some of its fat. Turn the chicken pieces over, season again, and cook until the other side is browned.

Put in the garlic cloves and the grapes. Put a lid on and cook over low heat for about 25 minutes until the chicken is very tender and cooked through, turning the pieces over at least once. The grapes should be very soft: some will burst and their juice mixed with the chicken fat will make a rich, delicious sauce. Taste and check the seasoning – you need salt and pepper to balance the sweetness of the grapes.

Basic polenta

You can make this in advance (it keeps for a long time in the fridge) and heat it through under the grill before serving.

Serves 4

900ml water

1 tsp salt

185g instant polenta

25g butter

black pepper

sunflower or olive oil, for brushing (optional)

In a large pan, bring the water to the boil with the salt. Add the polenta in a thin stream, whisking vigorously. When it comes back to the boil (it will gurgle and splatter), reduce the heat to very low and continue to stir for 2 minutes until it is very thick. Cover the pan and cook over very low heat for another 8 minutes, then stir in the butter and season with black pepper. Serve hot.

If you are making it in advance, pour the hot polenta into a large oiled tray, smooth the top and allow it to cool. When you are ready to serve, cut it into 4 squares. Brush the pieces with sunflower or olive oil and toast under a hot grill until very hot.

CHICKEN WITH WHITE WINE AND ROSEMARY

This is Italian and so simple. I was still working on this book in March 2020 and was retesting my recipes throughout lockdown while I was self-isolating. I kept ordering ingredients online and cooking and longing for someone to eat with me. Once, when my granddaughter Ruby arrived unexpectedly, I had just two chicken legs in the fridge and some fruity wine left in a bottle, so I made this. We sat in the garden at two separate tables. She loved it and asked me to put it in the book.

You can serve this with mashed potatoes or polenta (pages 228–9).

Serves 2

25g butter
1 tbsp extra virgin olive oil
2 chicken legs, bone in, skin on
200ml dry white wine
2 garlic cloves, cut in half
2 rosemary sprigs
½ tsp sugar
salt and black pepper

Heat the butter and oil in a sauté pan or frying pan, put in the chicken legs and cook over medium heat, turning the pieces to brown them all over.

Season with salt and pepper. Add the wine, garlic, rosemary and sugar, then cover and simmer for 30 minutes or until the chicken is very tender and cooked through.

Serve hot, pouring some of the sauce over your mashed potatoes or polenta.

CHICKEN WRAP INSPIRED BY THE FLAVOURS OF PALESTINIAN *MUSAKHAN*

I ate this famously sharp and spicy Palestinian chicken dish on flatbreads in Jerusalem and loved it. I made it for my granddaughters Sarah, Ruby and Nelly when we sat in the garden one night, and served it in tortilla wraps. They loved it too and enjoyed eating it in the wraps; they and their friends often eat like that. Serve with Greek-style yoghurt and cucumber and tomato salad (page 84). You can buy ground cardamom in Middle Eastern groceries.

Serves 6

3 large onions (about 600g), halved and thickly sliced

6 tbsp sunflower or olive oil

3–4 tsp sumac, or more to taste

2 tsp ground cinnamon

1 tsp ground allspice

*1 tsp ground cardamom
or 10 cardamom pods, cracked*

8 boneless skinless chicken thighs

6 large tortilla wraps

100g pine nuts or flaked almonds, lightly toasted

salt and black pepper

In a large frying pan or sauté pan, sauté the onions in 2 tablespoons of the oil over low heat with the lid on, stirring often and adding 1 teaspoon sumac, 1 teaspoon cinnamon, ½ teaspoon allspice, and some salt and pepper. Cook over low heat for 45 minutes. They should be gently caramelised by then. If they are not, remove the lid and turn up the heat to medium for a minute or so.

In another large frying pan or sauté pan, heat the remaining oil and stir in the remaining 2–3 teaspoons sumac, 1 teaspoon cinnamon, ½ teaspoon allspice and the cardamom. Open out the chicken thighs and put them in the pan, turning them in the spiced oil to coat them all over. Add some salt and pepper, then cook over low heat, with the lid on, turning the chicken pieces over at least once, for 15–20 minutes or until they are tender and cooked through.

Cut the chicken into bite-sized pieces and mix with the onions.

Heat the tortilla wraps as described on the packet. Put a tortilla on each plate. Spread some of the chicken and onion filling on one half and sprinkle with lightly toasted pine nuts or flaked almonds. Let everyone roll or simply fold their wraps.

CHICKEN AND ONION 'PIES' WITH MOROCCAN FLAVOURS

I have often enjoyed the Moroccan festive jewel in the crown *b'stilla*, a pigeon pie, and have made it many times myself, with chicken encased in layers of paper-thin pancakes (*warka*) or more often with filo pastry. Here, I have drawn from the flavours of versions from Fez (famously sweet) and Tetouan (famously sharp and lemony). A light rectangle of puff pastry sits in for the crust. It is both sumptuous and easy.

Serves 4

320g all-butter puff pastry sheet

1 egg yolk

2 large onions (about 430g), halved and thickly sliced

4 tbsp olive or sunflower oil, plus extra for greasing

¾ tsp ground ginger

1½ tsp ground cinnamon, plus extra to decorate

50g blanched almonds, coarsely chopped

6 boneless skinless chicken thigh fillets, cut into bite-sized pieces

1–2 tbsp lemon juice

grated zest of ½ orange

½ boiled lemon (page 226), chopped (optional)

icing sugar, to decorate

bunch (25g) of coriander, leaves chopped, to serve

salt and black pepper

Preheat the oven to 180°C/160°C fan/gas 4. Take the pastry out of the fridge about 20 minutes before you want to use it.

Unroll the pastry onto a lightly oiled baking sheet. Cut it into eight rectangles. Brush the tops with egg yolk mixed with a drop of water and bake for about 15–20 minutes or until the pastry has puffed up and is golden brown.

Put the onions in a wide frying pan with the oil, put the lid on and cook over low heat, stirring often, for about 10 minutes until they are very soft.

Stir in the ginger and cinnamon, then add the almonds and the chicken pieces and season with salt and pepper. Cook uncovered for 7–8 minutes, stirring and turning the chicken until it is tender and lightly browned. Add the lemon juice and orange zest, the boiled lemon, if using, and 3–4 tablespoons water, and continue to cook for 5 minutes.

Lightly cover the pastry rectangles with a dusting of icing sugar, and make a small lattice pattern with ground cinnamon on top.

Stir the coriander into the chicken mixture and serve hot. Place two puff pastry rectangles on the side of each plate.

CHICKEN WITH APRICOTS AND PISTACHIOS

Meat with fruit is a legacy of ancient Persia that spread through the Arab world. When Teuntje Klinkenberg, a friend in The Netherlands, asked me for a medieval Persian recipe with chicken for the National Museum of Ceramics, I looked in a translation of a thirteenth-century Arab culinary manual. I was intrigued by a dish of chicken with apricots and pistachios, a combination that is in my family and is trending with chefs today. I invited my brother Ellis and sister-in-law Gill, who live nearby, to eat my modern interpretation. It was fascinating to find that the flavours of the past are still with us today. Serve it with spiced rice (page 153).

Serves 4

2 tbsp sunflower oil

2 onions, chopped

8 chicken thighs, bone in, skin on

200g soft dried apricots

1 tsp ground cinnamon

1 tsp ground coriander

1 tbsp pomegranate molasses

juice of ½ lemon

75g pistachios, coarsely chopped

salt and black pepper

Heat the oil in a large sauté pan. Add the onions and cook over low heat, with the lid on, stirring often, for about 10 minutes until soft and golden. Take them out and set them aside.

Put the chicken thighs into the pan, skin-side down, add salt and pepper and cook over medium heat, with the lid on, for about 10 minutes until the skin releases its fat and the chicken pieces are well browned. Turn them over and cook the other side for 10 minutes, until browned, adding more salt and pepper.

Add the apricots and return the onions to the pan, lifting the chicken pieces so that they sit on top of the apricots and onions.

Measure 200ml water into a jug, stir in the cinnamon and coriander, the pomegranate molasses and lemon juice and pour over the chicken. Cook, covered, over low heat for 25 minutes until the chicken is very tender and cooked through and the liquid is reduced.

Serve sprinkled with pistachios.

CHICKEN WITH FREEKEH

The inspiration for this dish is my favourite Egyptian food: stuffed pigeon with freekeh, called *ferik* in Egypt. Freekeh is young green durum wheat that is harvested while still unripe and roasted in a pile in the open. The straw and chaff burns and the moist grain acquires a smoky flavour. It is then rubbed to remove the chaff. There are two commercial varieties: the whole grain and the most commonly sold cracked freekeh that cooks more quickly.

Egyptian pigeons are not at all like ours, with their dark meat and gamey flavour – they are more like French *pigeonneaux* or squabs. I use chicken instead of pigeon with freekeh. Do try my interpretation – it is wonderful and very easy.

In 1988, I was in Cairo to write about pigeons. Raising them is one of the great passions of Egypt. People raise them as carrier and racing pigeons, and for eating when they are tiny. I saw them peeking out of small mud brick dovecotes on rooftops and balconies and hanging out of windows. When I lived there, Cairo was like two cities with their backs to each other. The part I lived in was built by French and Italian architects; the other, with meandering streets and bazaars, mosques and mausoleums, was an old medieval Arab city. Rural Egypt was like an entirely different country, one that was centuries old. Now the entire city seemed swamped by the countryside. Millions of people had flooded in. There were flocks of sheep in the street, and chickens on the rooftops. I went to the *souk el hammam*, the pigeon market near the Citadel where hundreds of young boys and old men gather on Fridays to sell and exchange live birds. Some sat behind crates full of birds raised in farms outside the city, others stood holding only one or two. A few were selling very tiny baby ones for eating. Whenever it was on the menu I ordered stuffed pigeon. The stuffing varied, sometimes rice was used, with almonds or pine nuts.

Serves 6

2 large onions, halved and sliced

3–4 tbsp olive or sunflower oil

1 tsp ground cinnamon

¼ tsp ground allspice

½ tsp ground cardamom

6 boneless skinless chicken thighs

juice of ½–1 lemon

salt and black pepper

Freekeh

250g cracked freekeh

700ml chicken stock

½ tsp ground cinnamon

¼ tsp ground allspice

¼ tsp ground cardamom

35g raisins

3 tbsp sunflower oil or 30g butter

To serve

100g pine nuts, lightly toasted

1 tbsp sumac

400g Greek-style yoghurt mixed
with the juice of ½ lemon and a little salt

In a large frying pan or sauté pan, fry the onions in the oil over low heat with the lid on, stirring occasionally, for about 5 minutes until they begin to soften. Stir in the cinnamon, allspice and cardamom, and put in the chicken. Cook over low heat with the lid on, turning the chicken pieces a few times, stirring and adding salt and pepper, for about 30 minutes until the chicken is brown all over, very tender and cooked through, and the onions are very soft and brown. Cut each thigh into smaller pieces, add the lemon juice to taste and mix well.

While the chicken is cooking, wash the freekeh in plenty of water in a bowl. Pour off any chaff or burnt grains that float to the top, then drain.

Put the stock in a large pan with the cinnamon, allspice and cardamom and bring to the boil. Put in the freekeh, raisins, some salt and pepper, and stir well. Simmer over low heat with the lid on for about 20 minutes or until the grain is very tender and the liquid has been absorbed. If there is too much liquid left, remove the lid and let it evaporate. Stir in the oil or butter.

Serve the freekeh hot, with the chicken and onions on top, sprinkled with pine nuts and sumac and accompanied by the yoghurt.

CHICKEN IN A SPICY HONEY SAUCE BURIED IN VERMICELLI

We sat around a mountain of vermicelli decorated with chopped almonds and lines of cinnamon and icing sugar. Everyone helped themselves, digging in to find pieces of ever-so-tender baby pigeon in a rich aromatic sauce. From my memories of this stunning dish, I've come up with a modest interpretation of *shaariya medfouna* (it means 'buried in vermicelli'), a grand ceremonial dish of Fez. The savoury-sweet sauce is a legacy of the Moors banished from Spain, who settled in this most Andalusian of North African cities.

You can cook the chicken in its sauce in advance and heat it through when you cook the vermicelli just before serving. I make this in a wide double-handled pan that I bring to the table. You need short fine egg noodles for this dish or fine dry vermicelli nests (not rice vermicelli); they are sometimes sold as *capelli d'angelo* or angel hair pasta.

Serves 4–6

3 large onions, halved and sliced

4 tbsp olive oil

1½ tsp ground cinnamon, plus ½ tsp to garnish

¾ tsp ground ginger

good pinch of saffron threads

8 boneless skinless chicken thighs

1½ tbsp aromatic runny honey

1 tbsp orange blossom water (optional)

good pinch of chilli pepper (optional)

bunch (25g) of coriander or flat-leaf parsley, chopped

300g short fine egg noodles or dried vermicelli nests, crushed

40g butter

50g flaked almonds, lightly toasted

1 tsp icing sugar (optional)

salt and black pepper

In a heavy-based sauté pan wide enough to hold the chicken thighs in one layer, sauté the onions in the oil over low heat, with the lid on but stirring often, for about 10 minutes or until they begin to soften.

Add the cinnamon, ginger, saffron and salt and pepper and stir well. Put in the chicken and cook, covered, over low heat for about 8 minutes, stirring and turning the pieces of chicken over once.

Add about 250ml water and continue to cook, covered, over low heat for about 30 minutes until the chicken is very tender and cooked through and the onions are meltingly soft.

Cut the thighs in half. Stir in the honey and the orange blossom water, if using, and cook uncovered until the sauce is reduced and thickened, adding a little more water if it is too dry. Taste and adjust the seasoning: you need plenty of pepper or a touch of chilli to mitigate the sweetness. Mix in the coriander or parsley.

When you are ready to serve, cook the vermicelli in boiling salted water for 2–3 minutes, until al dente. Drain and return to the pan, stir in the butter and add salt to taste, if necessary. Spread the vermicelli all over the chicken and garnish with the flaked almonds, cinnamon and, if you like, icing sugar.

ROAST CHICKEN WITH BULGUR, RAISINS, CHESTNUTS AND PINE NUTS

When my grandchildren were small, I made regular weekly meals for all the family and it was always roast chicken. It was what the grandchildren wanted and it was easy to put three chickens in the oven together. Bulgur – whole wheat kernels that have been boiled, then dried and ground – is a rural staple in Turkey and the Arab world. You often see it drying on rooftops in the countryside there. With chestnuts, raisins, pine nuts and delicate spices, it makes a sophisticated accompaniment to the chicken.

Serves 4–6

1 large chicken
2 tbsp olive or sunflower oil
juice of ½ lemon
salt and black pepper

Bulgur pilaf

1 large onion, halved and sliced
2 tbsp olive or sunflower oil
500ml chicken stock (use 1 stockpot
or stock cube)
1½ tsp ground cinnamon
½ tsp ground allspice
½ tsp ground coriander

50g raisins, soaked in water
for 15 minutes
250g bulgur
50g butter, cut into pieces
50g pine nuts
100g cooked whole chestnuts, halved

Yoghurt sauce

200g Greek-style yoghurt
grated zest and juice of ½ lemon
grated zest of ½ orange
1 garlic clove, crushed (optional)

Preheat the oven to 200°C/180°C fan/gas 6.

Rub the chicken with the oil and lemon juice, salt and pepper and push the squeezed half lemon inside the cavity. Lay the chicken, breast-side down, in a baking dish and pour in about 5 tablespoons water. Roast for 1 hour then turn the chicken breast-side up and roast for another 15–20 minutes, until the skin is crisp and brown and the juices run clear when you cut into the bird between the leg and the body with a pointed knife.

While the chicken is in the oven, make the bulgur pilaf: in a large frying pan, fry the onion in the oil over medium heat, with the lid on, for about 20 minutes until brown and caramelised. Stir often and remove the lid towards the end.

At the same time, bring the chicken stock to the boil in a large pan. Stir in the cinnamon, allspice, coriander and some salt (taking into consideration the saltiness of the stock). Stir in the raisins and bulgur and cook over low heat, with the lid on, for about 10 minutes or until the liquid has been absorbed and the grain is tender. Fold in the butter, and add pepper, and more salt to taste.

Put the pine nuts and chestnuts in the frying pan with the fried onions and cook, stirring, for 2–3 minutes, then mix into the bulgur.

For the yoghurt sauce, beat the yoghurt with the rest of the ingredients with a fork.

To serve, cut the chicken into pieces and pour the lemony sauce that has formed at the bottom of the baking dish over the chicken and the bulgur. Serve with the yoghurt sauce.

ROAST DUCK LEGS WITH PEACHES

The legs are the most tender and juicy part of a duck. Rubbed with sweet spices, with a touch of honey melting on them at the end of roasting, and partnered with ripe peaches, they are sumptuous. You can find duck legs in most supermarkets. Check the roasting times suggested by the producer, as they depend on how fat the duck is. Serve them with potatoes roasted in the duck fat (see note opposite).

Serves 4

4 duck legs

2 tbsp olive oil

¾ tsp ground ginger

¾ tsp ground cinnamon

4 ripe peaches, cut in half and stones removed

125ml sweet Malaga wine or other sweet wine

2 tbsp aromatic runny honey, such as orange blossom or acacia

salt and black pepper

Preheat the oven to 180°C/160°C fan/gas 4.

Put the duck legs in a large baking dish, skin-side up, and prick them all over with a pointed knife to let the fat from under the skin run out.

In a little bowl, mix the oil with the ginger and cinnamon and plenty of salt and pepper, and rub some of this on each of the duck legs.

Roast for 50 minutes.

Take the dish out of the oven, lift out the duck legs and pour out some of the fat (pour it over the potatoes – see note). Return the duck legs to the dish, skin-side up, and put in the peaches, cut-sides up. Pour the wine over the peaches. Return to the oven and continue to cook for about 35 minutes.

Take the dish out of the oven, pour ½ tablespoon of honey over each leg and return to the oven for 5 minutes or until the peaches are soft, the duck skin is crisp and the meat is extremely soft and comes away from the bone easily.

Variation

Instead of peaches, use apricots – their sharpness cuts the richness of the duck meat.

Note

Have 1kg potatoes ready (I use Maris Piper). Peel them, cut them into large pieces and boil them in salted water for 10 minutes, then drain and shake them in a colander to roughen their surfaces and turn them into a baking tray. Pour on the hot duck fat and turn the pieces to coat them all over (add a little olive oil if there is not enough fat). Season with salt and put them in the oven to roast with the duck legs for the last 40 minutes of the cooking time, turning them over once.

MEAT PIES IN FILO PASTRY

When it comes to pies and wrapped foods, small is beautiful in the Arab world. For years I made tiny meat cigars and triangles. They were delightful finger food but labour-intensive and not what I want to spend time on today. I devised this pastry envelope with the flavours of Aleppo as a fun snack or light main dish to serve with a salad or together with a mixed vegetable dish. You need a tough type of filo pastry that does not tear easily (you will find it in supermarkets – I use a 270g box of 7 sheets measuring about 20 x 40cm). If your filo is very thin, you will need two layers with oil brushed between them for each parcel.

Serves 6

270g pack of filo pastry sheets
1 large onion, chopped
2 tbsp olive or sunflower oil, plus extra for brushing
500g lean minced beef
1 tsp ground cinnamon
½ tsp ground allspice
½ tsp ground ginger
2 tbsp pomegranate molasses
50g pine nuts, lightly toasted
large bunch (50g) of flat-leaf parsley, leaves chopped
1 egg yolk
2 tbsp sesame or nigella seeds
salt and black pepper

Take the pack of filo out of the fridge at least 30 minutes before you want to use it.

Fry the onion in the oil over medium–low heat for about 10 minutes until golden. Add the meat, some salt and pepper, the cinnamon, allspice and ginger and cook, breaking up the meat, crushing and turning it over until browned, for 8–10 minutes, adding the pomegranate molasses when the meat has begun to brown. Stir in the pine nuts and parsley and leave to cool.

Preheat the oven to 180°C/160°C fan/gas 4.

Divide the meat filling into six portions. Open out the filo sheets and keep them in a pile, covered with a tea towel, so that they don't dry out. Brush the top sheet very lightly with oil. Take a portion of filling and place it on the filo about 8cm from a short edge, forming it into a square shape, about 10cm square. Bring the short edge up over the filling to partially cover, then fold the long sides over. Carefully turn the parcel to completely enclose the filling, resulting in a square-shaped packet. Brush lightly with oil between any bits of filo. Repeat to make six pies.

Brush the pies with the egg yolk mixed with a drop of water and sprinkle with sesame or nigella seeds. Bake for 25 minutes or until the pastry is crisp and golden. Serve hot.

SPICY FRIED MINCED MEAT ON A BED OF AUBERGINE AND YOGHURT PURÉE

Turkish and Arab restaurants are primarily kebab houses that serve *mezzes*. The home-cooking equivalent of kofta kebab is fried minced meat. This interpretation of a Gaziantep speciality, with spices and pomegranate molasses, on a bed of creamy aubergine and yoghurt purée, qualifies as Middle Eastern haute cuisine.

My granddaughter Sarah cooked this for her Cambridge engineering tutor, Jossy Sayir. He is also a foodie. He came to lunch in my garden with his daughters and his guitar and sang – beautifully. We had promised to invite him when we heard that one of his aunts in Istanbul had given me recipes that went into one of my old books.

Serves 4–6

4 aubergines, about 1.25kg

500g Greek-style yoghurt

1–2 garlic cloves, crushed (optional)

2 large onions, coarsely chopped

4 tbsp olive or sunflower oil

500g minced beef

1½ tsp ground cinnamon

¾ tsp ground allspice

1½ tbsp pomegranate molasses

good pinch of chilli pepper (optional)

50g pine nuts, lightly toasted

large bunch (50g) of flat-leaf parsley, leaves chopped

a handful of pomegranate seeds to garnish (optional)

salt and black pepper

Preheat the grill to high. Prick each aubergine in several places with the point of a knife so that they don't burst when they cook. Place them on a baking sheet lined with foil. Cook under the grill for about 30 minutes, turning them at least once, until the skins are blistered and black in parts and they feel very soft when you press them. Peel them over a colander and chop and mash the flesh with a fork, letting the juices drain.

Put the yoghurt in a bowl. Add salt, pepper and the garlic, if using, and mix in the mashed aubergines.

In a wide frying pan or sauté pan, fry the onions in the oil over low heat, with the lid on, stirring often, for 20 minutes or until very soft and golden.

Add the meat, and cook, crushing, chopping and turning it over with a spatula until it changes colour. Add the cinnamon, allspice, pomegranate molasses, some salt and pepper, the chilli pepper, if using, and 4 tablespoons water. Cook for 15–20 minutes, stirring and turning the meat until it is very soft. Stir in the pine nuts and parsley.

Spread the aubergine and yoghurt purée in a serving dish and put the hot meat on top. If you like, sprinkle with pomegranate seeds.

MEATBALLS WITH SOUR CHERRIES

This is an old family dish that originates in Aleppo, Syria. In Egypt, my aunt Regine served it at her buffet parties on a bed of toasted pitta bread, cut into triangles. Her cook rolled the meat into tiny marble-sized balls. It was exquisite. Regine went on to live in Paris, where I saw her often; many of the recipes in my first book came from her. I use dried pitted sour cherries, if I can find them, and serve it on plain rice.

Serves 4

90g dried pitted sour cherries
300ml water
juice of ½ lemon, or more to taste
400g lean minced lamb
1½ tsp ground cinnamon

½ tsp ground allspice
3 tbsp olive or sunflower oil
1 large onion, halved and sliced
good pinch of chilli pepper (optional)
salt and black pepper

Put the dried cherries in a small pan with the water and the lemon juice, and simmer over low heat for 30 minutes until the cherries are very soft and the liquid has reduced, adding a little water if it becomes too dry.

Put the meat in a bowl, add the cinnamon, allspice and some salt and pepper, and use your hand to work to a soft paste. Take small pieces of the mixture, the size of a small walnut, and roll them into little balls between the palms of your hands.

In a large frying pan or sauté pan, heat the oil, add the onion and cook over low heat, stirring often, for about 5 minutes until it softens.

Push the onion to one side of the pan and put in the meatballs. Cook over medium–low heat for about 8–10 minutes, turning the meatballs to brown them all over, and stirring and turning the onion until golden.

Pour in the cherries with their liquid, season to taste with salt and pepper and a little chilli if you like, and simmer for 5 minutes. Serve hot, with rice.

PORK MEATBALLS WITH CURRANTS AND PINE NUTS IN A CIDER SAUCE WITH CHESTNUTS

My favourite pork dishes are roast belly of pork – I love the melting tenderness – and meatballs, because they absorb sauces well. For these, I was inspired by the French *sauté de porc au cidre* with chestnuts and by Sicilian meatballs that have raisins and pine nuts worked into the meat.

Serves 4

2 onions, halved and sliced

4 tbsp sunflower or olive oil

500g minced pork

good pinch of ground nutmeg

30g currants or raisins, soaked in water for 30 minutes

25g pine nuts

plain flour, to coat the meatballs

400ml medium-dry cider

180g pack cooked whole chestnuts

salt and black pepper

In a large sauté pan, fry the onions in the oil over low heat for about 10 minutes or until brown and beginning to caramelise, stirring often, then remove them from the pan.

Put the meat in a bowl. Add salt, pepper and nutmeg and knead vigorously to achieve a soft, paste-like texture. Work in the drained currants or raisins and the pine nuts. Take small pieces of the meat mixture and roll into little balls the size of a large walnut, pressing them firmly between the palms of your hands.

Roll the meatballs in flour, put them in the sauté pan and cook over medium heat, turning to lightly brown them all over. Add the cider and the chestnuts and return the fried onions to the pan. Simmer for 10–15 minutes, covered, adding salt and plenty of pepper and turning the meatballs over once, until they are cooked through. Serve hot.

TINY TENDER LAMB CUTLETS

A tour of kebab houses in Istanbul became a gastronomic marathon. At every stop I was invited (practically forced) to eat. At the fifth restaurant, they opened a big refrigerated room and showed me all the prize cuts, which were later presented to me straight from the fire on a gigantic tray. As well as the usual kebabs on skewers, there were baby lamb chops, kidneys, slices of calf's liver, beef steaks, *sucuk* (spicy beef sausages), and pieces of chicken. It was a gourmand's dream, but for someone sitting alone at a table, already satiated from eating elsewhere and afraid to give offence, it was a nightmare.

In restaurants, I always go for the minced meat kofta kebab, but my favourite to make at home are the tiny, ever-so-tender cutlets cut from a rack of lamb. I make them for my granddaughter Lily. They are her favourite, too.

I serve them with herby mashed potatoes with olive oil (use half the quantity on page 123) or cucumber and tomato salad (page 84). You can garnish with watercress or radishes.

Serves 2–3

1 rack of lamb (about 6–7 cutlets), trimmed
olive oil
salt and black pepper

Cut the rack of lamb into cutlets, using a cleaver or heavy knife. Brush them all over with about 1 tablespoon of olive oil.

Brush a griddle pan or heavy frying pan lightly with oil and heat over high heat. Cook the cutlets for 2–3 minutes on each side until they are brown on the outside but still pink and juicy inside. Do not overcook them: they are best eaten slightly underdone. The meat is so good all the cutlets need is salt and pepper.

PROVENÇALE DAUBE

This famous Provençal stew, with the mingled flavours and aromas of red wine, meat juices, garlic, orange peel, herbs and spices, is a marvellous winter dinner party dish. It is very easy to make and can be left gently simmering for several hours – you do not need to watch it – and you can make it the day before.

In the nineteenth century, every inn in Provence had a pot of *daube* in the ashes of the fireplace, ready for hungry travellers stopping on their way. It was served with potatoes, and in places with Italian settlers with polenta or small macaroni.

Lamb – shoulder trimmed of fat or neck fillet cut into large pieces – is the traditional meat for the daube, but you can use beef – topside, silverside, knuckle or cheek trimmed of fat. Serve with potatoes, polenta (pages 228–9) or short macaroni.

Serves 6–8

4 tbsp sunflower or olive oil

1–1.5kg lamb or beef (see introduction), cut into large pieces

2 large onions, each cut into 6 wedges

125g unsmoked pancetta or diced streaky bacon

5 garlic cloves, peeled

500g carrots, cut into slices 1½–2cm thick

1 bottle of red wine

2 bay leaves

4–5 thyme sprigs

1 tsp ground cinnamon

¾ tsp ground allspice

3–4 cloves

2–3 tsp sugar

strips of peel from 1 orange

3–4 tbsp cognac or grappa (optional)

salt and black pepper

Heat the oil in a large heavy-based pan or casserole over medium heat, put in the meat and cook, turning the pieces to brown them all over.

Remove the meat to a plate and put the onions and pancetta or bacon into the pan. Sauté for about 6 minutes, stirring until the onions are lightly coloured and the pancetta releases its fat. Add the garlic for the last minute or so, then the carrots, and season with salt and pepper.

Return the meat to the pan, pour in the wine and add the herbs and spices, sugar and orange peel. Add water to cover, bring to the boil, then turn down the heat to low, cover the pan, and simmer very gently (the *daube* should be barely trembling) for 2–3 hours, keeping the meat submerged, until it is so tender you can cut it with a spoon. Towards the end of the cooking time, remove the orange peel and, if you like, stir in the cognac or grappa.

BEAN STEW WITH CHORIZO AND BACON

My grandson Peter cooked this for us to test the recipe. The smell filled the house, and the taste… mmm. Spanish peasants used to dry their own beans and make their own chorizo with chopped pork meat and fat, garlic and *pimentón*, which gives it a reddish colour and strong distinctive flavour. There are many varieties of chorizo in different shapes and sizes, smoked or unsmoked, and with added herbs and seasonings. Fully cured chorizos are ready to eat; soft semi-cured ones need to be cooked. Any chorizo is great in this dish.

Serves 4

2 tbsp sunflower or olive oil

200g unsmoked bacon lardons or pancetta

1 large onion, coarsely chopped

4 garlic cloves, chopped

¾ tsp ground cinnamon

¼ tsp ground allspice

1 tomato, peeled and chopped

2 x 400g tins butter beans or cannellini beans, drained and rinsed

250g chorizo, soft semi-cured or fully cured, mild or hot, cut into slices

500ml chicken stock

4 thyme sprigs

salt

extra virgin olive oil, to serve

Heat the oil in a wide pan and put in the bacon or pancetta and the onion. Cook over medium heat for about 10 minutes, stirring and turning over occasionally with a spatula, until the bacon has released its fat and the onion is soft. Add the garlic and cook, stirring, until the onion is golden and the bacon crisp.

Stir in the cinnamon and allspice and add the tomato, beans and chorizo. Pour in the stock, add the thyme sprigs and simmer over low heat for 15 minutes.

Season with salt if necessary, bearing in mind that there is quite a bit of salt from the stock, the chorizo and the bacon. Serve hot and pass round the extra virgin olive oil for people to drizzle on.

LAMB WITH HONEY AND ROSEMARY

This is a very delicately flavoured stew: you would hardly know there was any honey. In Spain, they say *cordero al miel* came with the Moors. In North Africa, where the Moors (Iberian Muslims) settled after their expulsion from Spain, causing a culinary revolution, they say the combination of lamb with honey is Andalusian. Sweet with savoury is part of a Hispano-Arab style of cooking that developed during the centuries-long Muslim occupation of Spain. The South of France adopted the *carré d'agneau au miel et romarin*. My version is inspired by all three places. There is wine and just a touch of honey. A pinch of chilli is the Spanish way of mitigating sweetness.

Meat from the shoulder becomes meltingly tender without being stringy. A whole shoulder is very difficult to bone, so try to buy a boneless shoulder. Two lamb neck fillets will also do and need only 1 hour of cooking instead of the 2 hours for shoulder. Serve with boiled or mashed potatoes.

Serves 12

4 tbsp olive or sunflower oil

800g shallots, peeled

1 boneless shoulder of lamb, cut into large pieces

4 rosemary sprigs, leaves finely chopped

400ml dry white wine

3 tbsp brandy

1 tsp sugar

2 tbsp aromatic runny honey, such as orange blossom or acacia

salt and black pepper or chilli pepper, to taste

Heat the oil in a large heavy-based pan or casserole over medium heat. Put in the shallots and sauté for a few minutes, turning to brown them all over, then take them out and put them aside.

Cook the meat in batches in the same pan, turning the pieces to brown them all over. Return all the lamb to the pan, season with salt and sprinkle the rosemary in between layers of meat. Add the wine, brandy and sugar and cover with about 300ml water.

Bring to the boil then cover and simmer over low heat for 30 minutes. Put the browned shallots on top of the meat, add water to cover them, and continue to cook, covered, over low heat for 1–1½ hours until the meat is so tender you can cut it with a spoon. Ten minutes before the end, stir in the honey and some pepper or chilli pepper. Taste and add more salt if necessary.

SLOW-ROASTED SHOULDER OF LAMB WITH COUSCOUS, DATES AND ALMONDS

Shoulder of lamb is what I cook when I have many meat eaters to feed. Slow roasting makes the meat meltingly tender and juicy. I once made this shoulder with a date syrup glaze and couscous with dates for a dinner for the artist Michael Rakowitz. His sculpture on the fourth plinth in Trafalgar Square – representing the ancient statue of the Lamassu, the winged bull with a human head that was destroyed by ISIS in Iraq – was made out of empty date syrup tins. Dates have something of a sacred character in an Arab culture born in the desert. They symbolise hospitality and are said to have been a favourite food of the Prophet Muhammad. Their sweetness complements the sweetness of the meat. I love the combination.

I also serve slow-roasted shoulder of lamb with roasted vegetables (pages 122 or 129), and with the spiced rice on page 153.

Serves 6–8

1 whole bone-in shoulder of lamb

250g couscous

1 tbsp orange blossom water

1 tsp ground cinnamon

2 tbsp sunflower or vegetable oil

150g pitted dates, cut into small pieces

50g seedless raisins

100g blanched almonds, coarsely chopped

2 tbsp date syrup, plus more to pass around in the jar

65g butter, cut into small pieces

salt and black pepper

8–12 dates and 8–12 blanched almonds, to garnish

Preheat the oven to 240°C/220°C fan/gas 9.

Put the joint, skin-side up, in a baking dish or roasting tin, sprinkle with salt and pepper, and roast in the hot oven for 20 minutes. Then reduce the heat to 160°C/140°C fan/gas 3 and cook for 4 hours until the skin is crisp and brown and the meat is juicy and meltingly tender. Pour off the fat after about 2 hours.

Put the couscous in another baking dish, in which you can serve it. Add the same volume of warm water – about 300ml – mixed with a little salt, the orange blossom water and cinnamon, and pour it over the couscous, stirring well so that the water is absorbed evenly. Leave for about 10 minutes, then add the oil and rub the grains between your hands above the dish to aerate the couscous and break up any lumps.

Mix in the dates, raisins and chopped almonds, cover with foil, and put in the oven with the lamb for the last 20 minutes or until it is steaming hot.

Before serving, pour the date syrup over the meat. Stir the butter into the couscous so that it melts in and is absorbed evenly. With a fork, fluff up the couscous, breaking up any lumps. Add a little salt to taste, if necessary.

For the garnish, remove the stones from each date and replace them with the blanched almonds; decorate the couscous with these dates. Serve the meat with the couscous. Pass the date syrup around for people who may want some more.

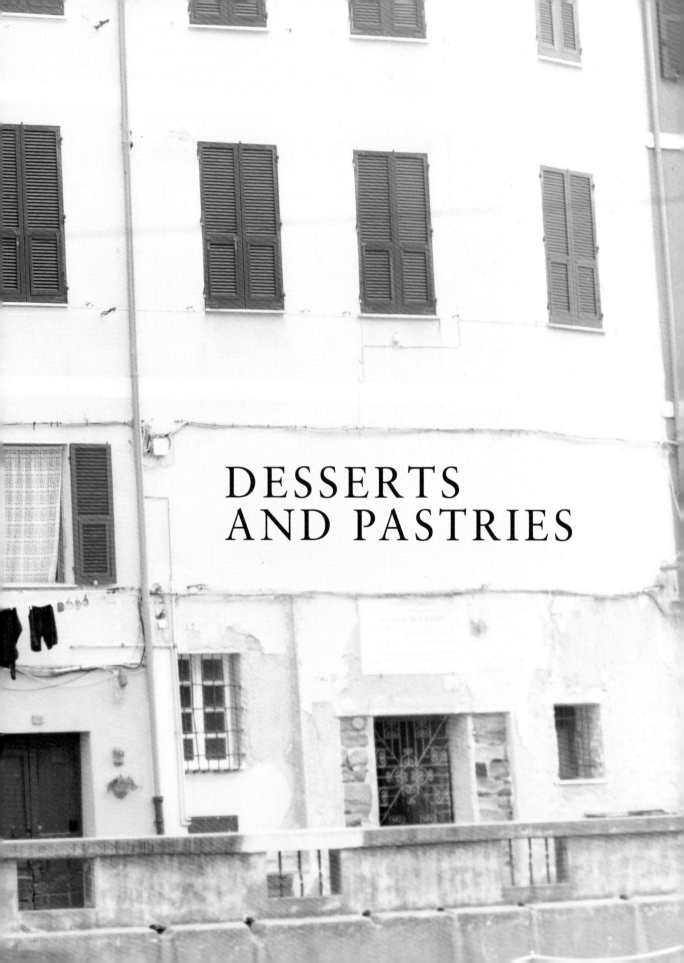

DESSERTS
AND PASTRIES

The traditional Mediterranean way of ending a meal is with fresh fruit. I like simply cutting up different types of fruit and arranging them in slices on a large platter or making a fruit salad. I often serve orange slices with Medjool dates and pistachios, sometimes with a drop of orange blossom water or a dusting of cinnamon. To serve with coffee or mint tea, I stuff pitted Medjool dates with walnut halves or with an almond or pistachio paste scented with rose water.

When I was a girl, the pastry I always longed for was a thick slice of bread soaked in caramel sugar syrup, topped with buffalo's milk cream so thick you could cut it with a knife. It is called *aish el saraya* (palace bread). I come from the sweet-toothed Arab Mediterranean world of filo and *kadaifi* pastries soaked in syrup, of candied fruits and fruit preserves and marzipan sweetmeats. I still make them – they are part of my happy childhood memories of visiting and entertaining and part of who I am.

But to end a meal, it is to France, Italy and Spain that I usually turn. Most of the desserts in this chapter are with fruit, and many – the tarts, compôtes, jellies, parfaits, chaussons, and the chestnuts in syrup – are French, inspired by what I eyed and often bought in patisseries and *traiteurs* in Paris. We can find all the Mediterranean fruits in Britain. Cooking them intensifies their flavours.

Arabs introduced milk puddings and almond pastries throughout the Mediterranean. You will find them in the following pages. But the flourless cakes with nuts and almonds are Passover cakes of the Sephardi Jews, whose ancestors, like mine, were banished from Spain and settled around the Mediterranean. They used ground nuts and almonds when their dietary laws forbade them flour or leaven.

FRESH BERRIES IN ORANGE CARAMEL SYRUP

Last summer, I managed to have regular deliveries of fresh berries straight from the farm. As a special dessert, I served them with an orange caramel syrup, which had an intense bitter-marmalade flavour, and orange-scented whipped cream.

Serves 4–6

500g mixed berries, such as raspberries, blueberries, blackberries, strawberries

250ml freshly squeezed orange juice

5 tbsp caster sugar

Keep the berries chilled in the fridge.

Heat the orange juice to boiling point.

Heat the sugar in a pan over low heat and watch it as it becomes liquid and gradually turns caramel brown. Don't let it get too dark or it will be bitter. Take the pan off the heat for a moment or two and then gradually pour in the hot orange juice, stirring vigorously to dissolve the caramel, which will have hardened. Put back over low heat for 3–4 minutes, stirring until the caramel is completely dissolved. Pour the syrup into a jug, leave to cool then chill, covered, in the fridge.

Before serving, rinse the berries briefly. Hull the strawberries, if using, and cut them in half. Serve the berries in a bowl, pour the orange caramel syrup over them and mix well.

Orange-flavoured whipped cream

Whisk 300ml double or whipping cream until firm, then whisk in 2 tablespoons caster sugar and the grated zest of 1 orange.

SWEET MUSCAT WINE JELLY WITH MUSCAT GRAPES

This grown-up jelly with jewel-like yellow and pink grapes is light and fresh with a deep flavour and intense aromatic scent. It is expensive but worth it for a special occasion.

Serves 4–6

5 gelatine leaves

375ml sweet Muscat or other dessert wine

300g Muscat grapes, washed

Soak the gelatine leaves in a bowl of cold water, separating them, for about 5 minutes until soft.

Heat the wine over gentle heat but do not bring it to the boil. Drain the gelatine leaves, squeeze out the excess water, and drop them into the hot wine, stirring vigorously until they have dissolved.

Rinse a mould with cold water. Pour in the liquid jelly and drop the grapes in. Let the jelly cool, then cover and put in the fridge to set for 4 hours or overnight.

When ready to serve, briefly lower the mould into a bowl of very hot water and then turn out onto a serving plate.

SANGRIA JELLY

This festive jelly is inspired by drinks I was served in a bar in Seville and it looks beautiful served in glass cups. It is great with port wine, but you can also make it with red or white wine, brandy or rum.

Serves 6

6 gelatine leaves
300ml port
300ml freshly squeezed orange juice
4 tbsp caster sugar
2 apples, peeled and cut into small pieces
2 peaches, peeled and cut into small pieces

Soak the gelatine leaves in a bowl of cold water, separating them, for about 5 minutes until soft.

Heat the port with the orange juice and sugar over gentle heat, stirring to dissolve the sugar, but do not bring it to the boil. Drain the gelatine leaves, squeeze out the excess water and drop them into the hot wine mixture, stirring vigorously until they have dissolved.

Put the apple and peach pieces in six cups or bowls and pour the liquid jelly over them. Let cool, then cover and put in the fridge to set for at least 4 hours or overnight.

CHESTNUTS IN SYRUP

This sophisticated dessert is my idea of heaven. It is incredibly quick to make with pre-cooked whole roasted chestnuts and is best done the day before or several hours in advance so that the chestnuts have time to absorb the alcohol. I use a very good cognac. I don't always use the whole amount of whipped cream to mix with the syrup, but keep some to float on coffee.

Serves 4

100g caster sugar

250ml water

½ tsp vanilla extract

180g pack cooked whole chestnuts

3 tbsp cognac or rum

300ml whipping cream

Put the sugar, water and vanilla in a pan and simmer over medium heat until the sugar has dissolved.

Add the chestnuts and cook for about 15 minutes until they are soft and the syrup is reduced. Lift the chestnuts out with a slotted spoon and put them in a small bowl. Pour in the cognac or rum and leave, covered, in the fridge. Keep the syrup in a separate container.

Whip the cream until it forms soft peaks, add the reserved syrup and whip until stiff. Serve with the chestnuts.

AMANDINES
ALMOND AND
PINE NUT PASTRIES

I got this recipe thirty-five years ago from a baker in a village called Lumières in Provence – he featured in the BBC TV series *Claudia Roden's Mediterranean Cookery*. The original recipe had 500g of sugar but many people now prefer less sugar – you can reduce the amount to 400g, depending on how sweet your tooth is. I still love it with 500g. It is the favourite offering I bring to get-togethers when there are a lot of people. It is very rich so I cut it into small pieces but people always want more.

Makes around 49 small pieces

1 tbsp sunflower or vegetable oil for greasing

6 eggs

400–500g caster sugar

500g ground almonds

200ml whole milk

½ tsp vanilla extract

5 drops almond extract

100g pine nuts

150ml apricot jelly or jam, to glaze (optional)

Preheat the oven to 180°C/160°C fan/gas 4. Line a shallow baking tin, about 30 x 30cm, with baking parchment and brush with the oil.

Using a fork, lightly beat the eggs with the sugar then add the ground almonds, milk, vanilla and almond extracts and mix thoroughly. Pour into the prepared tin. Sprinkle the pine nuts on top and bake for 1 hour or until the top is brown and the cake feels firm. If it is brown too early, cover the tin with foil.

If you wish, while the cake is still warm, melt the jelly or jam with 1–2 tablespoons of water and brush it over the top. Leave to cool.

To serve, cut into squares or rectangles with a sharp knife and lift out the amandines one by one.

QUINCE PURÉE

You can usually find quinces in Middle Eastern and Asian shops in the winter months. I keep them in the kitchen for days for their heavenly scent, and when I cook them the fragrance fills the house. Eating them like this, simply mashed with a little sugar, is pure joy. I serve the purée with the cream below, or with cheese – it is good with Pecorino sardo, Parmesan or Grana Padano, and with blue cheese or goats' cheese.

Serves 6–8

3 quinces (about 1.2kg total weight)
100g caster sugar

Preheat the oven to 150°C/130°C fan/gas 2.

Wash the quinces, scrubbing them if they have down on their skins. Put them on a foil-lined baking sheet and bake them for about 2 hours (the time depends on the size and ripeness of the fruit) or until they are soft enough that you can easily pierce through to the centre with a pointed knife. Leave them to cool.

Peel them, cut them in half and cut out the cores. It is messy but worth it. Put the flesh in a pan and cut it into pieces. Add the sugar and mash with a potato masher. Cook over low heat, stirring for about 5 minutes. Pour the purée into a serving dish and leave to cool, then cover and chill in the fridge.

Rose-flavoured whipped cream

Whisk 300ml double cream until almost firm, then stir in 2 tablespoons caster sugar and 2–3 teaspoons rose water and whisk until firm.

Alternatively, instead of rose water, add ¼ teaspoon vanilla extract.

APPLE *CHAUSSONS*

There are several pâtisseries near my studio on Rue Saint Dominique in Paris. One of them sells homely regional specialities and I can't resist heading there to get a *chausson aux pommes*. It is my guilty secret. My version is richer: I hope you will try it.

Makes 8 pastries

320g all-butter puff pastry sheet

4 apples

1 tbsp lemon juice

100ml pressed apple juice or water

50–60g caster sugar, to taste

4 egg yolks, plus 1 to glaze

80ml crème fraîche or double cream

sunflower oil for greasing

icing sugar for dusting

Take the puff pastry out of the fridge and out of its pack at least 20 minutes before you want to use it so that it is pliable and does not crack when you unroll it.

Peel, core and quarter the apples, dropping them into a bowl of water with the lemon juice to stop them discolouring. Drain them and put them in a pan with the apple juice or water, put the lid on and cook over low heat for 10–15 minutes until they are very soft. Remove the lid and simmer for a few minutes until all the liquid has evaporated.

Mash the apples with a potato masher, stir in the sugar, and cook over medium heat, stirring, for about 2–3 minutes to allow more liquid to evaporate.

Beat the 4 egg yolks with the crème fraîche or double cream. Add this to the apple purée and cook over low heat, stirring vigorously, for 1–2 minutes until the mixture thickens slightly. Leave it to cool.

Preheat the oven to 200°C/180°C fan/gas 6 and lightly oil a large baking sheet. Mix the remaining egg yolk with a drop of water.

Unroll the pastry onto the baking sheet and cut it into eight rectangles. Lightly brush the tops with the egg yolk glaze and bake for 20 minutes until puffed up and browned.

Leave the pastries to cool slightly, then slice them through the middle with a serrated knife and fill each one with about 2 heaped tablespoons of the apple cream. Dust with icing sugar.

SWEET CHEESE MILLEFEUILLES

These are like the apple *chaussons* (page 282) but with a cheese filling. They should be eaten hot or warm. You can make them in advance and reheat before serving. Eat them with your hands, like a sandwich.

Makes 8 pastries

320g all-butter puff pastry sheet
sunflower oil for greasing
1 large egg, plus 1 yolk
250g mozzarella (not di bufala)
50–60g caster sugar
grated zest of 1 orange
icing sugar for dusting

Take the puff pastry out of the fridge and out of its pack at least 20 minutes before you want to use it so that it is pliable and does not crack when you unroll it.

Preheat the oven to 200°C/180°C fan/gas 6. Lightly oil a large baking sheet. Mix the egg yolk with a drop of water.

Unroll the pastry onto the baking sheet and cut it into eight rectangles. Lightly brush the tops with a little of the egg yolk glaze and bake for 10 minutes until puffed up and lightly browned. Leave to cool slightly.

For the filling, cut the mozzarella into pieces and blend to a creamy paste with the sugar, orange zest and the whole egg.

When the pastries have cooled a little, slice them through the middle with a serrated knife and fill each one with about 2 tablespoons of the filling. Turn them over, brush the new tops with the remaining egg yolk glaze and bake for about 15 minutes until browned.

Serve hot, turned over again and dusted with icing sugar.

APPLE PARFAIT WITH CALVADOS OR RUM

I buy Calvados, the apple brandy, mainly to put in apple desserts, such as crumbles, omelettes and pancakes. Its sweet aroma adds to the pleasure of this lovely frozen dessert. A parfait does not need to be churned.

Serves 6

4 Golden Delicious apples, peeled, cored and sliced
150ml dry white wine
100g caster sugar
3 egg yolks
3 tbsp Calvados or rum
150ml double cream

Put the apples and the wine in a pan and simmer, covered, over low heat for 5–10 minutes until the apples are soft.

Remove the lid and raise the heat. Add half the sugar, mash the apples with a potato masher or fork, and cook, stirring, until the apple purée is thick and most of the liquid has disappeared.

Beat the egg yolks with the remaining sugar until thick and pale. Pour into the apple purée, off the heat, stirring vigorously, then stir over low heat for 30 seconds. Stir in the calvados or rum, leave to cool, then chill in the fridge.

Whip the double cream until firm and fold into the cold apple purée. Line a bowl with clingfilm (it makes turning out easier) and pour in the apple mixture. Cover the top with clingfilm and freeze overnight.

Serve straight from the freezer. Remove the covering clingfilm, turn out on a serving plate, and remove the remaining clingfilm.

Variation

~ Pears may be used instead of apples, with kirsch or Poire William.

PARFAIT MOCHA PRALINÉ

This very easy no-churn ice cream has the wonderful mix of coffee and praline flavours that I love and also brings back many happy memories. The same ingredients, plus sponge fingers, were those of a cake my mother always made for my father's birthday. When I went back to Egypt for the first time after 30 years, I looked in the window of the old pastry shop near where I used to live and there was the French cake book open at the page with our *diplomate mocha praliné*. My mother had ordered it there and learnt to make it herself after she left Egypt.

Serves 8–10

50g blanched hazelnuts

50g caster sugar

300ml double cream

175g sweetened condensed milk

2 tbsp instant espresso coffee powder

To make the praline, in a dry frying pan (not a non-stick one) toast the hazelnuts over medium heat, shaking the pan, until they just begin to colour. Tip the hazelnuts onto a plate and set aside.

Put the sugar in the pan, spread it out and place over medium heat until it becomes liquid and turns a light golden colour (watch it as it can quickly turn very dark and bitter.) Put the hazelnuts back in and turn them around until they are well coated with the liquid caramel. When the caramel turns brown, pour it onto a baking sheet lined with baking parchment (or onto an oiled baking sheet). Let it cool completely. When it is hard and brittle, grind in a food processor.

Whisk the cream with the condensed milk and coffee powder until soft peaks form. Fold in the praline, keeping 2 tablespoons aside to decorate. Keep this in a little cup covered with clingfilm until you are ready to serve.

Line a mould with clingfilm (it makes turning out easier) and pour in the cream mixture. Cover the top with clingfilm and freeze for at least 6 hours or overnight.

Take out of the freezer 15 minutes before serving. Dip the mould into a bowl of very hot water for a few seconds. Remove the covering clingfilm. Turn the mould upside down onto a serving plate and remove the remaining clingfilm. Serve sprinkled with the reserved praline.

ROAST PEACHES WITH SWEET WINE, CLOTTED CREAM AND CARAMELISED PISTACHIOS

When the fruits we buy have not ripened on a tree, roasting is a way of bringing out the most they can offer. The sensual pleasure of this combination of roasted peaches with clotted cream and caramelised pistachios is immense. Use ripe but not soft peaches.

Serves 4

4 peaches, unpeeled, cut in half and stones removed

120ml sweet white wine

60g caster sugar

60g pistachios

113g pot of clotted cream

Preheat the oven to 190°C/170°C fan/gas 5.

Arrange the peaches in a shallow baking dish, cut-sides up. Pour the sweet wine over them, so that a little settles in the hollows. Roast for about 30 minutes (the time depends on the size and ripeness of the fruit) until very tender when you pierce one with a pointed knife. Let them cool, then chill, covered, in the fridge.

For the caramelised pistachios, line a baking sheet with baking parchment. Heat the sugar in a small pan over medium heat and watch it as it becomes liquid and gradually turns brown, the colour of dark honey. Don't let it get too dark.

Quickly put in the pistachios and stir until they are entirely coated with caramel, then pour onto the lined baking sheet. Leave to cool completely. When the caramel is cold, hard and brittle, lift it off the baking sheet and coarsely chop.

To serve, spread some clotted cream over each half peach and sprinkle with caramelised pistachios.

Variations

~ Instead of sweet wine, use dry white wine and 1–2 tablespoons sugar.

~ Instead of clotted cream, use whipped cream or a good Greek-style yoghurt.

NADIA'S GRANITAS

My daughter Nadia, an artist, designer and film animator, was named 'Ice Princess' in New York when she wrote a book, *Granita Magic*, and sold her home-made ice lollies in High Line Park, a garden built on a disused overhead railway line over Manhattan. Now that she lives in London she makes granitas for the family and creates ice lolly recipes for my grandson Cesar's Ice Kitchen.

Each granita serves 6–8

Orange and lemon

300ml water

140g caster sugar

900ml freshly squeezed orange juice (from about 6–7 oranges)

50ml lemon juice (from 1 lemon)

1 tbsp orange blossom water

Pear and anise

300ml water

3 star anise

100g caster sugar

juice of 1 lemon

5 flavourful pears, peeled, cut into eighths and cored (about 600g flesh)

Milk and honey

800ml whole milk

6–7 tbsp honey

4 cardamom pods, crushed

2 tbsp rose water

To make the orange and lemon granita mixture, put the water and sugar in a small pan and simmer just until the sugar dissolves. Take off the heat and stir in the fresh orange and lemon juices and the orange blossom water.

To make the pear and anise granita mixture, put the water, star anise, sugar and lemon juice in a pan and add the pears. Bring to the boil, then gently simmer, covered, for about 5–8 minutes until the pears are tender. Take off the heat and leave to cool for at least 20 minutes. Remove the star anise and blend the mixture to a smooth purée.

To make the milk and honey granita mixture, put 200ml of the milk, the honey and the crushed cardamom pods in a small pan and gently simmer, stirring just until the honey dissolves. Take off the heat and leave to infuse for 20 minutes. Strain the milk mixture into a bowl, discarding the cardamom. Pour in the remaining milk and the rose water.

Whichever granita you are making, pour the granita mixture into a wide, shallow container, cover and freeze for 3–4 hours, then scrape and crush the ice with a fork. Repeat this process every hour or so, at least three times, until the mixture has turned into small sequin-like ice flakes.

Before serving, rake the granita up again with a fork to lighten the texture. It's best eaten within a day or two, but will stay fresh for longer in an airtight freezer container. The pear and anise granita is also nice served with cream.

ANDALUSIAN RAISIN AND SWEET WINE ICE CREAM

I discovered this splendid ice cream when I was researching the cuisines of Spain. Raisins soaked in sweet dark wine are mixed into the rich vanilla ice cream when it is almost firm and the same wine is passed round for pouring over.

Serves 10 or more

100g raisins or currants

1 bottle of sweet Pedro Ximénez sherry or Malaga Moscatel wine

700ml double cream

300ml whole milk

1 small cinnamon stick

few drops vanilla extract

8 large egg yolks

100g caster sugar

Put the raisins in a small bowl, pour in 100ml of the sherry or wine and leave to soak.

In your not-quite-largest pan, heat the cream and milk with the cinnamon stick and vanilla until almost boiling. Remove from the heat and leave for 30 minutes to infuse before removing the cinnamon stick. Reheat the milk.

Using an electric whisk, beat the egg yolks with the sugar until pale and thick. Add a ladleful of hot milk and whisk well, then pour the mixture into the milk pan, off the heat, stirring vigorously with a wooden spoon. Now place the pan in a larger pan of boiling water over medium heat, and stir constantly until the mixture thickens enough to coat the spoon. Do not let it boil or it will curdle. (If it does curdle you can save the ice cream by beating thoroughly with the electric whisk until it is smooth.)

Pour the custard into a serving bowl and let it cool, then cover with clingfilm and put it into the freezer. After about 3–3½ hours, when it is firm but not yet hard, take it out of the freezer and mix in the raisins together with their sherry or wine. You must do this before the ice cream becomes too hard to mix but is firm enough so that the raisins remain suspended evenly and do not sink to the bottom. If you do not mix thoroughly there will be little white lumps in the ice cream but that too is lovely. If you want to serve the ice cream turned out onto a plate, transfer the custard to a mould lined with clingfilm and cover. Return it to the freezer for at least 6 hours or overnight.

To serve, take the ice cream out of the freezer. Remove the covering and dip the mould into a bowl of hot water for a few seconds. Turn the mould upside down on the serving plate and remove the remaining clingfilm.

Pass round the bottle of Pedro Ximénez or sweet wine for everyone to drizzle a little over their ice cream.

RICE PUDDING WITH FRUIT IN SYRUP

Rice pudding is much loved everywhere around the Mediterranean in a variety of flavours – vanilla, orange zest, cinnamon, cardamom, honey. I love them all, but I have a special affection for mastic. It gives this pudding a delicious and intriguing taste. Mastic is the resin from a tree which grows on the Greek island of Chios. You can buy it in small 'grains' or crystals in Greek and Middle Eastern stores. You have to crush and grind them to a powder with ½ teaspoon sugar, using a pestle and mortar. Use very little, otherwise the taste is unpleasant. The variation with cardamom is great too.

Serves 8–10

150g round Italian or pudding rice

350ml water

1 litre milk

100–150g caster sugar, to taste

2 tbsp rose water

½ tsp ground mastic (from about 4 mastic crystals)

50g pistachios, chopped

Fruits poached in syrup

150g caster sugar

500ml water

1 tsp lemon juice

½ tsp vanilla extract

12 cardamom pods, cracked

4 pears, peeled, quartered and cored

8 apricots or greengages, cut in half and stones removed

Put the rice in a large pan with the water. Bring to the boil and simmer for 8 minutes or until the water has been absorbed. Then add the milk and simmer over very low heat, stirring occasionally, for 35 minutes until the rice is very soft. Add 100g of the sugar and cook, stirring until dissolved. Taste and add more sugar if necessary. There should still be some liquid in the pan (the pudding will firm as it cools and should be very creamy). Add the rose water and vigorously stir in the mastic then take off the heat. Pour into a shallow serving dish and leave to cool. To serve, sprinkle with chopped pistachios.

For the poached fruits, put the sugar and water in a pan with the lemon juice and bring to a simmer. Add the vanilla and cardamom. Drop in the pears and simmer for 8 minutes, or until just tender (the time depends on their ripeness). Add the apricots or greengages and cook for 2 minutes more. Lift the fruit out of the syrup onto a plate, to remove the excess syrup. Serve at room temperature, with the rice pudding.

Variation

Omit the mastic and add 10 cracked cardamom pods at the same time as the milk.

LEMON TART

Around the corner from my studio in Paris, I stop to buy a *tarte au citron* at the pâtisserie in the Rue de Bourgogne. My version has an intensely lemony *crème au citron* filling. It is worth making the sweet biscuity *pâte sucrée* if you have time, but if you are in a hurry you can use a good bought sweet shortcrust pastry or pre-cooked pastry case.

Serves 6–8

Sweet shortcrust pastry

200g plain flour, plus extra for dusting

50g icing sugar

100g cold unsalted butter, cut into pieces, plus extra for greasing

1 large egg yolk

Lemon filling

85g unsalted butter

grated zest of 1 lemon

75ml lemon juice (2–3 lemons)

120g caster sugar

2 large eggs

To make the pastry, mix the flour and icing sugar in a bowl. Using your fingertips, rub the butter into the flour until crumbly. Stir in the egg yolk with a fork. If the dough is still dry, stir in 1–2 tablespoons cold water until it holds together. Press it into a ball, flatten it and wrap it in clingfilm or greaseproof paper, then chill for 30 minutes.

Preheat the oven to 200°C/180°C fan/gas 6 and lightly grease a 23cm round tart tin.

Roll out the dough on a lightly floured surface, turning it over once and dusting with flour underneath. Use your rolling pin to lift the dough and lay it into the prepared tin, pressing it firmly into the sides. Alternatively, you might find it easier with this soft dough to line the tin by simply pressing in lumps of dough with the palm of your hand. Trim off any excess pastry and prick all over the bottom of the pastry with a fork. Bake for 12–15 minutes, or until golden brown and biscuity.

For the lemon filling, melt the butter in a heavy-based pan. Take the pan off the heat and add the lemon zest, lemon juice, sugar and eggs. Whisking vigorously, bring to a simmer over low heat, and continue beating for 30 seconds more as it thickens. Cover and leave in the fridge until ready to use.

Leave the pastry case to cool, then pour in the filling and chill before serving.

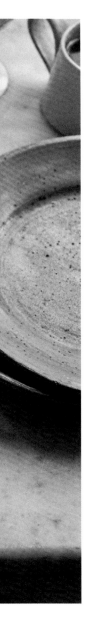

PLUM CLAFOUTIS

I have often made clafoutis over the years. For this book, I tried this famous French baked dessert again with different fruits and batters. When cherries, the traditional fruit, were in season, I didn't want to cook them. They were too good and too expensive. I just wanted to eat them. My favourite clafoutis was with greengages or plums in a light custard perfumed with vanilla and rum. I hope you will love it too.

Serves 6–8

butter for greasing
800g plums or greengages
120ml milk
120ml double cream
4 large eggs
100g caster sugar
1 tbsp plain flour
½ tsp vanilla extract
3 tbsp rum
1 tbsp icing sugar for dusting

Preheat the oven to 180°C/160°C fan/gas 4. Butter a 28cm shallow baking dish.

Wash and dry the plums or greengages, cut them in half and remove the stones. Arrange them cut-side down in the baking dish, where they should fit snugly.

Bring the milk and cream to the boil in a pan, then remove from the heat.

Beat the eggs with the sugar and flour until well blended, then add the vanilla and rum. Pour the hot milk into the mixture, whisking continuously, then pour over the fruit.

Bake for 45 minutes or until set. Serve warm, dusted with icing sugar. It's best eaten warm, not hot.

ALMOND PUDDING WITH APRICOT COMPOTE

Milk puddings thickened with cornflour are traditional dishes with an old history in almost every country around the Mediterranean. There are also versions with added ground almonds. This is the Sicilian *biancomangiare di mandorle*, with a floral perfume and subtle bitter-almond flavour, paired with a sharp apricot compote.

Serves 6–8

500ml whole milk

35g cornflour

100g caster sugar

50g ground almonds

25g pistachios, finely chopped

3–4 drops (not more) almond extract

1½ tbsp orange blossom or rose water

Apricot compote

1kg apricots, cut in half and stones removed

150ml water

100g sugar

1 tsp vanilla extract

Pour 400ml of the milk into a pan and bring to a simmer. Mix the cornflour with the remaining 100ml of cold milk, stirring vigorously until it is completely dissolved.

As the milk in the pan reaches simmering point, lower the heat and vigorously whisk in the milk and cornflour mixture. Continue to whisk constantly for 2–3 minutes until it comes back to a simmer and becomes a thick cream.

Add the sugar, ground almonds, pistachios and almond extract and continue to cook over low heat for 12 minutes. Stir in the orange blossom or rose water and pour into individual glass bowls or cups. Chill, covered in the fridge.

For the compote, put the apricots, cut-side up, in a wide pan with a tight-fitting lid, adding the water and sprinkling the sugar between the layers. Put the lid on and put the pan over high heat. The apricots will soften in about 5 minutes and produce a lot of juice. Add the vanilla and continue to cook with the lid off, stirring often, for another 5 minutes until the apricots have collapsed. Leave to cool. If you are making it in advance, keep covered in the fridge.

When serving, spoon some apricot compote on top of the almond cream.

YOGHURT CAKE

This Turkish cake is like a light, airy, fresh-tasting cheesecake. We make it all the time in my family and you really must try it.

Serves 6–8

butter or sunflower oil for greasing
4 large eggs, separated
100g caster sugar
3 tbsp plain flour
400g full-fat Greek-style yoghurt
grated zest and juice of 1 unwaxed lemon

Preheat the oven to 180°C/160°C fan/gas 4. Butter or oil a round non-stick cake tin (about 23cm in diameter) with a removable base.

Using an electric whisk, whisk the egg whites until soft peaks form.

In another bowl, using the same whisk, beat the egg yolks with the sugar until thick and pale. Add the flour, yoghurt, lemon zest and juice and beat to a homogenous cream.

Gently fold the egg whites into the yoghurt mixture and pour into the prepared tin. Bake for 40–45 minutes, until the top is lightly browned – watch it carefully for the last few minutes of cooking so that it doesn't brown too much. The cake will puff up like a soufflé and then subside.

Let it cool a little before lifting it out onto a serving plate. Serve warm or cold.

Macerated strawberries

For a beautiful accompaniment to the yoghurt cake, briefly rinse 500g strawberries, hull and cut them in half through the stem end, then sprinkle with 60g caster sugar and the juice of ½ lemon and leave for 1 hour.

HAZELNUT CAKE WITH CHOCOLATE GANACHE

Hazelnuts and chocolate are traditional partners and they work beautifully here in this hazelnut cake topped with a thick layer of luscious chocolate ganache. If you don't have a 20cm cake tin you can use a larger one; I have also made this in a 23cm tin.

Serves 12

butter for greasing
plain flour for dusting
6 large egg whites
75g caster sugar
250g blanched hazelnuts, coarsely ground

Ganache

300ml double cream
*200g best-quality dark chocolate (70 per cent cocoa solids),
broken into pieces*

Preheat the oven to 180°C/160°C fan/gas 4. Butter a 20cm round non-stick cake tin with a removable base and dust with flour.

Using an electric whisk, whisk the egg whites until stiff then gradually and gently fold in the sugar and the ground hazelnuts.

Pour the mixture into the prepared tin and bake for 45–60 minutes until pale golden and firm to the touch.

Leave to cool before lifting it out of the tin.

For the ganache, pour the cream into a pan and heat to boiling point, then take off the heat. Put in the chocolate and leave for 5 minutes until it softens, then beat with a whisk or a spatula until thoroughly blended. Spread over the cake generously.

CHOCOLATE CAKE

Our all-time favourite family birthday cake is a Sephardi Jewish Passover cake. I had the recipe from my mother's friend Lucie Ades, whose family came from France and was of Spanish ancestry. I am guessing that they were from Bayonne in South West France, where Jews fleeing the Inquisition in the early sixteenth century settled and started the first chocolate manufacturing industry. It is there that chocolate and cakes with almonds first appeared. I have always made this with the Menier Chocolat Patissier that I find at my supermarket. Serve it with double cream or whipped cream.

Serves 12

butter for greasing

plain flour for dusting

200g best-quality dark chocolate for cooking, broken into pieces

6 large eggs, separated

75g caster sugar

100g ground almonds

icing sugar for dusting (optional)

double or whipped cream, to serve

Preheat the oven to 180°C/160°C fan/gas 4. Butter a 23cm round non-stick cake tin with a removable base and dust with flour.

Melt the chocolate in a heatproof bowl placed over a pan of boiling water so that the bowl does not touch the water.

Using an electric whisk, whisk the egg whites until stiff.

In another bowl, using the same whisk, beat the egg yolks with the sugar until pale. Mix in the ground almonds and then the melted chocolate. Add a few tablespoons of the beaten whites and mix them in to loosen the very dense almond and chocolate mixture, then fold in the remaining whites.

Pour the mixture into the prepared tin and bake for 30 minutes or until firm to the touch.

Leave to cool before removing from the tin. Dust with icing sugar, if you like, and serve with double cream or whipped cream.

WALNUT CAKE

This cake is as delicious as it is simple, with a pure walnut flavour complemented by an orange fragrance – a traditional Mediterranean combination. You must make sure the walnuts aren't stale, as they have a tendency to become rancid. These quantities give a thin cake, about 2cm thick – you can double them if you want a larger cake, using a 25cm or 28cm round tin. It is a perfect quick tea-time cake.

Serves 4–6

butter for greasing
125g walnuts
2 large eggs
125g caster sugar
grated zest of 1 orange
icing sugar for dusting

Preheat the oven to 200°C/180°C fan/gas 6. Butter a 22cm round non-stick cake tin or tart tin with a removable base.

Put the walnuts in a food processor and grind, not too finely; set aside.

Using an electric whisk, beat the eggs with the sugar until pale and thick. Add the orange zest and then fold in the walnuts until well mixed.

Pour the mixture into the prepared tin and bake for 40 minutes or until firm to the touch.

Leave to cool before removing from the tin. Dust with icing sugar before serving.

I thank the friends who came to dinner over the years and helped me choose the recipes that went into this book. My family have always been regulars at my table, and in the final months before handing in the manuscript, my children and grandchildren offered to test recipes. Everyone took to cooking passionately. Their names are in my dedication. Thank you all for your feedback and enthusiasm. You have helped make the book what it is.

My warmest thanks go to the friends far away who offered to test recipes. I appreciated their checking and comments hugely. The writer Adina Hoffman in New Haven, Connecticut, whom I got to know at Yale, also gave an American perspective. I often turned to her and her husband the poet Peter Cole for general advice. Jonah Freud, who is translating *Med* into Dutch and is the owner of the best cookbook shop in Amsterdam, tested while on a canal journey in France. She is a fantastic cook and food writer, as well as a fount of culinary knowledge for chefs and food writers who come to her for advice. Gabrielle Sachs, who is married to my cousin Dov and lives in Bordeaux, is a cardiology nurse renowned for her cooking and the most passionate home cook I know. She brought a French lens to the recipes and was my 'super tester'. I could hardly keep up with her requests for more recipes to try and waited for her comments and suggestions, hoping for a '*délicieux! Dov a adoré*'.

I am more grateful than I can say to my agent Lizzy Kremer for her warm friendship and unstinting support over many years, and for her encouragement, advice and championing of this book. Thank you also for testing recipes Lizzy; your comments were a great help. Working with you is a huge privilege and a joy. I thank Maddalena Cavaciuti, Lizzy's assistant at David Higham, for testing too. I valued her Italian know-how.

I am thrilled and delighted with the beautiful book Ebury has produced and thank Andrew Goodfellow, Lizzy Gray, Laura Higginson and Celia Palazzo for wanting to make it the best it could be. I feel lucky and grateful to be published by you. I have special thanks for Andrew for the title, and for Celia, my editor, for making it all happen and for bringing together the dream team that created it. I have many thanks too for Emily Brickell, who took over when Celia left to have her baby.

I am full of admiration and especially grateful to Emily Preece-Morrison, the indefatigable editor and project manager, for her care and dedication, for the brilliant way she captured the spirit of the book, inspired the creative team and got it all to work. I thank the copy editor Maggie Ramsay for her eagle eye and attention to detail; Frankie Unsworth, the amazing food and props stylist, for creating the feel of the Mediterranean for the shoots and to her assistant Izy Hossack for the cooking.

I love Susan Bell's lyrical photography. She has a magic touch. Her photos of food are both simple and seductive and make you want to cook. Her seascapes and scenery are moving and make you happy even if you cannot go there. I love Dave Brown's engaging design and the way he used the sea and landscape and enmeshed the beautiful photos from all over the Mediterranean, some of them his own, in a poetic net. Thank you Susan and Dave for turning the book into a work of art.

I have many thanks too for the Ebury team who worked on the production, sales and marketing of *Med*: Lucy Harrison, Stephenie Naulls, Claire Scott, Antony De Rienzo and Fiona Atkinson; and for Vanessa Forbes and Anjali Nathani for deftly handling the foreign editions, Anjali also for setting up the Frankfurt Book Fair meeting.

As I cooked through *Med*, I thought affectionately of people I got to know in different countries while researching their food, especially those who cooked for me, taught me and showed me around. They allowed me into their lives and came into mine. I am still in touch with many – we call, visit and stay. I am forever grateful to them for enriching my life with so much more than recipes.

PHOTOGRAPHIC CREDITS

All photography by Susan Bell, except where credited below:

pp. 28, 158, 159, 213, 216, 238–239, 265 © Claudia Roden; pp. 4–5, 70 top, 86–87, 114–15, 138–9 © Dave Brown; pp. 74, 96, 97, 140, 170–1, 176, 206–7, 260 © Alamy; pp. 220–1 © Getty/iStock

1

Ebury Press, an imprint of Ebury Publishing,
20 Vauxhall Bridge Road,
London SW1V 2SA

Ebury Press is part of the Penguin Random House group of companies whose addresses
can be found at global.penguinrandomhouse.com

First published by Ebury Press in 2021

www.penguin.co.uk

A CIP catalogue record for this book is available from the British Library

ISBN 9781529108583

Design: Dave Brown at Ape Inc. Ltd
Photography: Susan Bell, except where otherwise credited (see page 319)
Food and prop styling: Frankie Unsworth

Colour origination by Altaimage Ltd, London
Printed and bound in Italy by Graphicom

Penguin Random House is committed to a sustainable future for our business, our readers
and our planet. This book is made from Forest Stewardship Council® certified paper.